UNSTOPPABLE

CHALLENGE ACCEPTED

VOLUME I

TARIKU BOGALE

UNSTOPPABLE

Dual Publisher © 2017 by Tariku Bogale

ISBN: 978-0-9982934-0-0

Made In The USA

CONTENTS

PART IV
A GLOBAL BUSINESS MOGUL LANDS IN THE HOLLYWOOD

DURING MY PRESCHOOL YEARS, the northeast African country was caught in a famine so great thousands of people died. The civil war that had begun in the decades before my birth would rage through my first ten years, leaving devastating scars that would take a long time to heal. My childhood was tough, but so was I. I drew strength from all these adverse circumstances, from my faith, from the people who showed me love, and from the angels watching over me.

Despite all the many hardships I saw and nearly impossible challenges I would encounter, I always chose hope and goodness for the way forward. I was instilled at an early age with a love of books and learning and was blessed to have the company of young Peace Corps workers, who gave me a view of the larger world that could open itself up to me, if only I had the will and determination to seek it out. This bigger world encompassed far more than fruit stalls, coffee plantations, and the limited offering and opportunities of my small, dusty village. Instead of these things, beyond these things, they showed me a world that was mine to explore, inhabit, and inspire.

PART I

From a Struggle for Survival to a Race to the Top

CHAPTER ONE:

Leaving the Jungle, and Struggling to Make a Life through Education

MY FAMILY LIVED in the Amaro Mountains in Southern Ethiopia, where lions, leopards, and hyenas roamed freely and we could hear their sounds from distance and sometimes the hyenas could be heard nearby.

My mother went into labor early and was told that I was dead in utero, so they had to drive to a major city to have surgery. It was over 400 kilometers, or nearly 250 miles, a very long journey for a couple expecting a difficult medical procedure and a tragic result, but since our little village of Amaro had no electricity, there were no other options for this kind of emergency medical procedure but to travel: the first stopover being Dilla dust town, in vain to find a specialist for surgery, then heading to the capital city of Ethiopia, Addis Ababa, and landing in Black Lion Hospital, a state owned hospital.

My parents were overjoyed and felt very blessed at the end of this terrifying ordeal to find that their son was alive and healthy. They named me Tariku, which means "the story," perhaps because the way I came into the world was such a dramatic, heart-stopping story for them. I also like to think it is because I will have many stories to tell over my life, good stories that will help and inspire others.

My father was angry at my mother because he believed she had married him for his money. He ended their marriage in court by divorce decree, whereupon she received a financial settlement and he left my other siblings in her care, abandoning them to her.

My father claimed that he was not my siblings' father. He kept me away from my mother, even though I was just a little boy who was too young to understand these things. He prohibited me from seeing her and would frighten me by telling me that my mom might try to kill me. I remember that for many days and weeks, perhaps months, I could not stop crying because of how much I missed my mother and my siblings.

Finally, one day the neighbors took pity on me and arranged to help me go visit my mother in secret. I can see now that it made them very sad to see such a small boy so heartbroken over the separation from his mother. They reminded my father not to treat me in such ways, as one day when I grew up I might not forgive him.

After that, I was sent to live in my father's mother's house in Amaro. By age four on the recommendation of the church school (Creche) I was admitted to grade one and promoted very quickly through first, second, and third grade within a one-year school term when my father decided to relocate me to Dilla on the advice my grandmother to receive better schooling. He sent me $10 per month to cover my food and other expenses, which only covered my food (dinner and lunch), and had to figure out from age eight for other expenses such as clothes and shoes.

I liked to think about things, to learn about the world, and I loved being challenged to solve a problem. When I was in fifth grade, I got the highest scores in the entire school. Still, because I lived apart from my mother, sisters, and brother, there was no one in my family there to congratulate me and share pride in my accomplishments.

This was not the case with the other students. Many of my peers had families that were more present in their lives. It was hard for me, just a young boy of eight or nine, to see others warmly encouraged by their parents and family members, and have no one there to offer the same. I did not blame them for this, but it stuck with me and made me seek out and value strong connections. That part of my childhood was an exciting time, because I loved to learn, but it was a lonely time, too. I knew I would want something different for my own family when I grew up.

Ninth grade was a turning point for me. I was 12 years old. My mother, my two brothers, and my sister were suffering. They were struggling to find enough money to buy food to eat and had no place to stay and nothing to eat most of the time. I had to bring them to where I was staying. This angered my father, since I did not consult him about it.

Before they came to live with me, I had been caught up with older kids, doing drugs and alcohol and other things. Because they knew I had a room of my own, they would use me for the room to do unsavory things. But by the time my family came, I knew I had to stop. I had to focus on the future.

My father stopped sending me the monthly $10, but every now and then, he would help me—take me for something to eat, give me some money. He did not want to punish me; he was just upset that I had brought my mother and siblings in and he was not asked about it.

There were American Peace Corps members in Dilla. They used to come teach math, science, and other subjects in the school. Because I was on the streets a lot, I was accessible to them; I would go to parties and bars with them, and I would show them the way around the town. But they taught me much more—they taught me how to be responsible, they taught me about family. They came all the way here, alone, without their families. They would talk about missing their relatives and how far away they were; they showed me the importance of family and what it meant to sacrifice.

Through seeing their pictures and hearing their stories, and being a shoulder for them to cry on, I became conscious about the meaning of family. Even if we could not always understand each other, it was feelings, not words that mattered.

In ninth grade, I would bring some of my Peace Corps friends to my home. They told me about scholarships and programs at colleges and universities in the United States, especially the University of Florida. By that point, I had become involved in causes at school, like AIDS awareness and environmental causes. I became a voice at my school about social issues. My friends in the Peace Corps planted the idea of making a difference in the world in my head, and so I started thinking about writing to universities for an application.

I wrote to schools and environmental organizations as far as Norway—the Peace Corps members gave me addresses. One of those places was the University of Florida. I communicated with the University of Florida for more than two years. The dean of the school saw the drive I had and saw I could inspire others and put me in touch with families in my town that I could inspire.

He invited me to come to Florida, and I asked my

father for help. I had to go to Addis Ababa in order to fax the University of Florida to let them know I was going to come, and my father gave me money to go to the capital city.

When I got to Addis Ababa, I was in line to send the fax to University of Florida when an attractive young lady came up behind me. She looked very tired, and I told her she could go ahead of me. She thanked me and did so. I introduced myself, and she told me her name was Fiona. She waited until I was done sending my fax and then told me it would be faster if I sent emails to the university.

I explained that I did not have access to the Internet, so she took me to an Internet café. This was 1998, and in Ethiopia not many people had computers yet. She opened an email account for me, and from there we began to get to know one another. We spent the next few days together.

I went back to Dilla and since I did not have a phone, I had given Fiona my neighbor's phone number. She called and said she wanted to come visit, and I picked her up halfway from Addis where we first met.

Fiona went back to my village with me and we spent six weeks together. There were a lot of expectations in my town; with my family and friends expectations were high, because she was a white woman and British.

We got engaged: she was 26, and she did not realize how young I was, 14. She asked me to take her to the Kenyan border because she was touring Africa. Eventually, she sent me an email from London that she was not interested in me anymore and broke it off. I was devastated. I did not tell my family because the expectations they had had for us were too high; I did not want to disappoint them.

I finished high school, but my heart was not in it. I was not focused after Fiona ended things. I did not have the grades to go to college just then, but I knew I would go to school in the future.

■ ■ ■

Growing up, I wanted to be a doctor. If you asked me when I was young, I would have told you that I wanted to practice medicine to help people. This was in large part because of my mother's health problems. After the surgery she had when I was born, my mother was never the same. She had many medical problems, and while her symptoms would subside, they never really went away. I wanted very badly to help her.

However, there was a change of plans. I enrolled in Hilcoe Computer Academy in 1999, in Addis Ababa. My father refused to help me financially because he was still under the impression that I would be getting support from Fiona. Even though we had broken off our engagement, I had not shared that with him. I was too upset and humiliated that the relationship had ended. I would walk to school because I had no money for transportation. It was five kilometers each way.

The dean took notice of my perseverance and positive spirits and took me under his wing. I reminded him a little of himself when he was younger, the dean said. Many students were older, in their 50s and 60s, learning how to use computers so that they could change careers, so I was the youngest student there.

He was very impressed with me and wanted to encourage me to further my studies and make a success of myself. I will always remember his encouragement. It is because he encouraged me that I want to reach out to young people and encourage them.

Despite the help I received from the dean of the computer academy, things were not easy for me there in Addis Ababa, and eventually, I dropped out and went to Peak, a repair school, where I met Cliff, the American-educated owner.

■ ■ ■

I don't know how I afforded any of this; I feel I have had angels watching out for me my entire life. I never had any money, but people would meet me in the street or random coffee shops and give me money and pay my bills. I had a lot of help.

Eventually, I met Bahiru, an older man who became my friend. He was a lecturer in computer science at University of Addis Ababa, and he started giving me pocket money. With that, I eventually set up a business called ACT, Advanced Computer Technology. My family was still pressuring me to help support them and I hoped my new business venture would allow me to contribute to their well-being. My father was still not adequately caring for my mother and my siblings. He was not a dutiful man and he did not support them. They struggled to get by, and often did not have enough to eat and struggled to get clean water.

Eventually, I went back to Dilla, where I met another Peace Corps member, a white woman. She had her own home, and she asked me to come over to Wonago, 12 kilometers away from Dilla, so I had to rent a motorbike to impress while not knowing how to ride. It was a Honda 125 cc and not easy to start the engine, as it was worn out and old.

While I was busy helping her to furnish her home. She told me to go to South Africa—that I would be successful there and do well there, with a good future. I think she thought this because I was very confident with white people. South Africa was coming out of apartheid and not everyone was comfortable with white people.

I went to my father and lied. I told him Fiona was in Kenya, we were engaged, and I needed to go to Kenya to be with her. He gave me $300. After giving my family money for food, I ended up at the Kenyan border, broke.

■ ■ ■

I had no money, and my father wouldn't give me any more. I somehow was able to get on a plane and found myself in Nairobi. I still wore the ring from my engagement to Fiona, but in Nairobi, I sold it. I was sad to see it go but I needed the money. With the proceeds from the ring, I stayed in downtown Nairobi, in a hostel, with backpackers I had met on my journey. I was traveling on very little, staying in backpacker places, learning things about how to live and travel cheaply.

I had a job for a time, training people to use computers. But more than that I wanted to travel and to get to South Africa as the Peace Corps woman had suggested, but I needed a visa because I held an Ethiopian passport. One of the backpackers told me that I would be able to cross the border easily if I had a Kenyan or Tanzanian passport, since they enable free movement.

I became friends with conductors on buses, and I met someone who got me a fake Tanzanian passport so I could pass into Dar es Salaam, the capital of Tanzania. It was a falsified passport with my picture on it. Even though I did not speak the language there, I made friends in Dar es Salaam. People were interested in me. It was perhaps telling that I drew people to me, and they made the effort to communicate with me despite our language barriers.

I continued to learn from backpackers about cheap places to stay and ways to make travel easier. Then, after two months in Dar es Salaam, living in a hostel, I was running out of money. My father could send me money from Ethiopia via the hawala brokers, an old and well-established system of money transfers in use in the Middle East and parts of Africa. I would have to cross the border again and return to Nairobi to get it, so I went, leaving my bags in my room in Dar es Salaam.

■ ■ ■

At that time, Kenya was very dangerous. I had felt much safer during my short stay in Dar es Salaam, so I did not want to stay very long in Nairobi. I had left my bags in the hostel back in Dar es Salaam and wanted to go back and eventually travel to South Africa, so I crossed the border again with my fake Tanzanian passport into Tanzania.

When I went back to the hostel to check in, I spent a long time in friendly conversation with the woman at the front desk: she really liked me, and we laughed and joked together. I remember there were two men watching.

I think the men were jealous of our easy rapport because maybe they liked her, too, or maybe they suspected that because I was traveling I would have a lot of money, even though that was far from the truth. The next morning, the police came. Someone had tipped them off that I was not Tanzanian and was carrying a fake Tanzanian passport. The police demanded a bribe from me, 50,000 shillings, about $25. I did not have that kind of money and I was angered that they would target me. I refused.

Immediately, the police arrested me and put me into the back of a police van. I was in the van with a lot of guys. Just like that, everything changed. As soon as I got into the van, there were guys there who were bigger and more powerful. They started removing my belt and my shoes. There are organized gangs in prisons and oftentimes even the men who have just been arrested already have connections to these gangs. You have to submit to them, for your own safety. I had very nice Timberland shoes. They were good for trekking, very sturdy shoes, and also fashionable, as I learned from Peace Corps volunteers and backpackers.

■ ■ ■

The tough guys in the prison van took the Timberlands from me, along with everything else that had value. It was crowded and stuffy in there. There must have been 30 people in that van.

We went straight to the courts for trial. I was dazed from how quickly everything was happening. I did not understand what was going on. Just a little while ago, I was enjoying a relaxed life in a hostel, but here I was under arrest. On top of that, everything was in Swahili and I did not speak a word of it. There were no interpreters to translate for me. It was all very fast and very confusing.

Before I knew it, I had been given a six-month prison sentence. This, for the "crime" of traveling somewhere to make a better life with one kind of government document and not another. When I think about it now, I know how wrong that is. At the time I was confused, disoriented, and anxious about my sudden reduction in circumstances and the dangers I might face in the jail.

Because I had struggled so much already in my life, I was able find the resources in me to face this ordeal without fear. Even though I was alone in this, I had been alone before and learned to handle myself with tough characters and to survive with few resources beyond my wits. I kept my head down and set about learning the best ways to survive in the prison.

CHAPTER TWO:

Strength in the Mind,
Even When the Body Is Confined

EVEN WITH this mind-set, prison was tough for me for the first two weeks—I was crying nonstop and depressed. It was a lot to adjust to. The prison was in the middle of a desert and used to be a work camp for slaves and a holding cell for slaves before transit. It was a very old prison, with many, many prisoners.

We slept head to toe, 30 men in one room. There was no toilet, just a bucket. Anything that happened in that room, everyone could hear and see—and all the things that usually happen in prisons took place all the time. There was no window, no sheet, just a clean cement floor. Because Dar es Salaam is near the ocean, it could be too hot or too cold. Either way, we were crammed into that room and sharing just the clean cement for a bed. We ate twice a day. Breakfast was a corn porridge that had to be eaten hot, for it became quite bitter when it cooled and gave off a sour, distasteful smell. There wasn't even any salt to improve the taste.

It became apparent rather soon that I would have to make some decisions about whom I would ally myself with in the prison. This was 2000, two years after the coordinated bombings of the US embassies in Nairobi and Dar es Salaam, and here I was in a prison in Dar es Salaam. There were Muslims who visited the prison, bringing extra food, some personal items like a hairbrush or toothbrush to give to Muslim prisoners.

■ ■ ■

There were many foreigners in the prison who found it helpful to convert to Islam so that they would be comforted in this way, but I did not want that. I had been raised in the Ethiopian Orthodox Christian Church and I knew my heart and my faith. Also, I was wary of the terrorist activity that had led to the bombing and I did not want to mistakenly fall in with people who might have such expectations of me.

Even though I knew I could get bail if I converted to Islam—for just as Somalis came nearly every day to the prison to bail out other Somalis, so would Muslims post bail for Muslim prisoners—it felt right to me that I remain true to my own faith. I have always felt this way, instinctively. You might say I don't know any other way than to be honest about who I am. I like to try many things, but I am always true to my heart, and in my heart I was a Christian. I have been going to church since I was 12 years old. I was 16 in 2000, and my faith had become an important part of my identity.

In addition to the religious people coming to the prison, it was also clear that organized criminals active in the drug trade corridor that ran through Dar es Salaam could bail me out. There was a lot of drug trade in Dar es Salaam, and a lot of the men in the prison were there for that. They were mules who had had drugs surgically implanted into their bodies. They did not swallow packets of drugs like most of the mules you hear about in the US. They had surgeons put it in their bodies and close it up. Mostly they came from Pakistan.

I think they mostly dealt in cocaine, but it could have been heroin, too. There were a lot of foreigners, including Pakistanis and Bangladeshis, in the prison and they were mostly there for drug-trafficking offenses. They would also offer gifts, as well as the possibility of bail.

I could have walked out of the prison and had a car to meet me, but then I would have owed my freedom to some very bad people, who would in turn expect me to help them do things with which I wanted no involvement.

I had heard of the sorts of things these men were capable of. I had traveled through some dangerous parts of the world already, at that young age, and knew I wanted no part of this. As much as I might want my freedom sooner, or to have some small comforting items, I resolved to stay strong, to take care of myself as best I could, and bide my time until my release.

I also knew there were others in the prison who were offering gifts because they wanted to begin a sexual relationship. This is very common in prisons, as is well known, and at night it was clear that in the cell there were men who had paired off with other men. That was not my way, to go with another man, so I made sure to refuse those gifts as well so there would be no confusion about that.

I was a bit suspicious of what others might want of me, so it seemed best not to make any alliances until I knew more about how the place operated. Above all, I did not want to owe anything to anyone there. I was also very wary of the food, because there were stories of chemicals being mixed into it to weaken the body and make the prisoners sick. I was very careful. I kept to myself, and I did what I could to observe what was happening. I had learned about the ways of the street from when I was a young boy, looking after myself, so I had some understanding of how to take care of myself in this situation.

■ ■ ■

The other prisoners thought I was very strange, but some of them admired me, I think. They could see that I was an educated person and that I wanted more for myself. I was determined not to be set back even though I was living in such bleak conditions. I knew I had fallen afoul of the authorities, and, yes, I had broken the law, but the law itself was ridiculous. Why should good people who want opportunities be prevented from crossing borders to make a better life for themselves?

As if to show my determination to keep my mind active, I decided I would act as if I still had an office and stick with my expertise as a computer specialist. I was worried that I would lose touch with my profession and I was determined that that would not happen. One day, I built a keyboard out of wood. I would sit practicing on it, every day a little, to keep my mind active.

The other prisoners laughed at me, but I knew that if I stuck with this I would remember my dreams and keep them alive. Maybe they laughed, but maybe they also chose to commit more crimes. I did not choose to go that way. The keyboard I made and the daily practice I did with it is a good example of the kind of work I did to focus my mind when my life was not where I wanted it to be. This is my habit in difficult times and it has saved me many times.

Every day, all the prisoners had to work to keep the prison running. I did not mind having to work because it gave me something to do to keep myself busy during those long lonely months locked away. There were many foreigners like me in Dar es Salaam who had also been arrested and jailed for traveling with improper documents or no documents at all.

■ ■ ■

These foreigners, like me, were put to work cleaning. Tanzanian prisoners did farm labor, which was much more difficult, backbreaking work. The cleaning work I did was very dusty. The dust made my eyes itch and water. It clogged my nose and filled my lungs. I developed a hacking cough. I also had to lift very heavy things. I had to carry 25 liters of water. It was very hard work. I was weary from the effort, exhausted at times, and my strength was leaving me.

There were guards in the prison who noticed me and looked kindly on me, as well as some of the long-term prisoners on death row who had a bit of status. They told me that as a foreigner I should not have been assigned such a difficult job. They noticed my cough and said that I should tell the prison authorities that I had asthma.

The prison authorities sent me to a doctor who examined me and confirmed the asthma. After that, my duties were made lighter. I no longer had to clean the dustiest parts of the prison. I also received better rations with more bread and more milk for breakfast.

My strength began to return. I became friendly with the Tanzanian national boxing champion, known as Cash Boy. He was often kept in handcuffs, even at his ankles, because he had managed to escape the prison numerous times. He was linked to drug trafficking in southern Africa, especially in South Africa, Johannesburg, Hillbrow. Cash Boy was in prison because he had killed someone in a fight in a club. I knew a friend and associate of Cash Boy, Snake Eye, who was held for drug trafficking. Cash Boy taught me the importance of training the body and kickboxing.

■ ■ ■

Also in the prison with me was a Portuguese guy in his middle 60s who shared his previous luxury life and numerous houses around the world including in Italy and Portugal who claimed to have children around my age, and that was why he was eager to look after me. He was caught moving five tons of cocaine. He had four years remaining on his sentence. He was highly connected and often bribed the guards for special privileges. I think he had probably bribed someone to get a lighter sentence, too.

He would share with me his copies of English-language magazines like *Time* and *Newsweek* because he knew I was educated and liked to read. He knew that I was not going to join the drug trade, but that did not stop him from trying to win me over to it. By then I had been there long enough to know what small acts of friendship would incur no serious debts. I could read his magazines and not worry that he would expect me to join his criminal enterprise. We became almost like friends because we understood one another. When I left the prison, he had a car and driver waiting for me. I had one more chance to join him in his work, and probably make a lot of money doing it, but I was sure of myself and my path in life, and once more I refused.

After I got out of the prison, I was free.

CHAPTER THREE:

Entrepreneur and a Lawyer, Almost

IN JOHANNESBURG I started a computer business. I ran an Internet café on the second floor of a city building. I had large offices, with an extra office I rented out to another computer professional. People would come to use the Internet, to have their computer repaired or updated, and to purchase or repair their mobile phones, which were very new at the time.

I was friendly with a beautiful woman who had a restaurant that took up the first floor of the building where my business was. Her name was Billie. Billie was very good looking and was the center of attention in any group. She dressed at the height of fashion and attracted a very smart, chic crowd to her restaurant. Billie's cousin was also very close to me, as was his wife, who was a very shrewd businesswoman named Selam.

I had a deep affection for Billie and I thought we saw a shared vision of a life together. But I could not say anything to her about this. She was quit coy, and she used her single status to draw wealthy and stylish people to her restaurant. Billie's restaurant in Johannesburg was a chic place to hang out, in part because Billie was very stylish.

■ ■ ■

There was a lot of competition for her attention, and she knew how to make that work for her business. People wanted to be around her, so that made her restaurant very fashionable, too. There was a lot of competition from other men for her attention. She was a start-up person, and she attracted a lot of stylish people with money to her restaurant.

Billie allowed me to have my 17th birthday party in her restaurant. I invited all my friends to come to the restaurant to celebrate. I was residing in the penthouse on the top floor of the same building, the only residential unit in the building, so it was very quiet.

At the party, I was looking very stylish. At the appropriate moment, I gave a toast. In the toast I started to thank people for coming, naming each of the important people in my life. Of course, I named Billie, and I said, spontaneously and quite honestly, without thinking of what might come as a result, "I love her." This made Billie's cousin very angry! I think it surprised Billie, too, a little.

Maybe it did not surprise her to find out that I felt this way but that I said it all of a sudden, so publicly, and to such a large group of our mutual friends. Well, this was something else! When Billie's cousin got angry, a huge fight broke out. Another cousin hit me with a pool cue. Everyone was trying to hold the cousin back from beating me. It was very tense and dramatic.

Ermy was Selam's husband, who was very successful in business. She was very smart and in some ways was a mentor to me. She was really something! She took a lot of risks but was very smart. She used to send people to Europe and the US. They were asylum seekers.

It's a very common thing in Africa, when people get a good education and then after leaving school, there is no opportunity for them in Africa, and they seek asylum in the West, preferably in London or New York.

If you could get through border control at the airport in Johannesburg, you could get off the plane in New York or London and immediately apply for asylum, and then there was a chance you could stay. But you had to get through border control in Johannesburg first and arrive there in order to do it. Johannesburg was a big point of embarkation for asylum seekers arriving in the US and Europe by air from Africa. Selam knew people at the airport. She had connections there. She would send Ethio-pian people to the airport in Johannesburg and they would count on her connections to allow them onto the plane.

At that time that I hung out at Billie's restaurant; I had a three-bedroom penthouse on top of the building. It was the only residential unit, so it was very quiet and very special. My business was on the second floor, right above the restaurant. I took on a roommate, though, who pushed me out of the apartment. He made a side deal with the landlord. I was renting a room to him but charging him the entire cost of the rent. He found out and made a deal with the landlord, and they told me the apartment was his and I did not live there anymore! It still amuses me today to think of the things people would do.

■ ■ ■

There was another guy who did computer training in my office on the second floor there. He also pushed me out in the same way. I rented a room to him in my office for his training and he decided he wanted the whole lease, so he went to the landlord. It was a similar thing, and a common thing that happened in business. I was not happy but I did not feel too bad about it either because it was a thing that people did. It also showed that I had chosen good spaces and built them up so that other people desired them.

I had a friend from Pretoria, Dereje, who was very highly skilled in computers. He came to my penthouse immediately after the fight and tried to console me. I was very upset and confused about what had happened. I was only making an honest statement to my friends at a time of celebration and paying tribute to a woman I thought I was going to be with.

It shocked me that there would be anyone who would come to celebrate my birthday who would not wish for me—for us—to have that happiness. Dereje was very sympathetic. He insisted that I not remain there alone, in such close proximity to Billie and to her cousin who had attacked me. He took me home to Pretoria by taxi that night, giving everyone time to calm down. I stayed there two days. Meanwhile, back in Johannesburg, everyone wanted to find the guy who started the fight.

I was in an unusual position in Johannesburg as an entrepreneur, running my own small computer business at a very young age. Most of the people I knew had no opportunity for them. They were hawking things on the street for a living. These were highly skilled people who could have done other jobs, but there was nothing like that there.

■ ■ ■

It is not an easy life, hawking things. You have to carry things out into the street. You have to work very actively all day, calling out to the customers to attract them to your wares. You are on your feet all day long, and when you are finished, you have to carry those same things home with you at night. The work is very physically taxing; it is not an easy life.

As a small businessman, I had the comfort of working in an office that I called my own. I took pride in that, in having a nice office to show to customers and all the world. I was able to use my wits in my work, my cleverness about computers and about customers, to make some small and growing success in the world. In those days, not a lot of people had computers or knew about how to use them, but very soon everyone wanted to have one, and even for those who could not afford to have one at home, communicating by email was becoming more and more the norm. I had a vision when I opened that business, for the future, for where things were going. Soon after that I was providing a vital service to the community. It gave me status and success at a young age.

I did training for people learning to use their computers, which made my business in high demand for a lot of different kinds of customers. I did all the flyers for important local concerts. All the best promoters worked with me. I also worked with Selam on the asylum cases.

Other people I knew got stuck hawking, but I had a vision of a way I could build a better life. I was the only one in that community who had a vision. But I did not look down on people. I felt badly for them that they had to work so hard, to tire themselves and sweat to make a living.

■ ■ ■

I realized I could help them by writing their asylum cases, so that when they got off the plane in New York or London, they would have the case already written up to make their claim. Most of the asylum seekers are eco-nomic, and people were eager to have help in moving to the West, where they could have more opportunities and a better life. I also was able to team up with Selam, who was a very smart businesswoman and who mentored me. People were very grateful to have this service, and we were able to help a lot of clients.

My landlord in Johannesburg was a Taiwanese guy, Mr. Wong. He was about 65 or 70 years old. He had bought the building. His parents had settled in Johannesburg and he had grown up there. He would see me driving a nice car or wearing nice clothes and raise my rent. Then one day, I came back and he had put all my things on the street, all of my furniture. He had rented the office suite to someone else. I took the few things of value and left the rest. This was soon after the fight at my birthday party and I was ready to move on to something else. I decided I was going to go to London and start again.

The most valuable item I had in my business was my four-in-one printer and a diary I kept while I was in high school. The four-in-one was a very expensive item in those days. It printed, scanned, faxed, and did photocopies. I gave it to my cousin to hold onto and I decided to go to London to seek asylum. I would go without papers and count on Chris and his connections to get me through. I was working with a Nigerian guy at the time, Chris— we had done some deals.

He decided he was going to leave and he offered to send me to London. I sent a message to Billie, because she had been so special to me. I wanted her to know that I was moving on with my life, that I wished her well in her business and in her future, and that she should move on with hers, too. It was only fair to her to say goodbye after all we had done together.

I did not feel badly that we were parting ways. For her, I think it was business: she was able to attract so many wealthy and stylish young men to her restaurant because she was single and could flirt with them. I told everyone I was leaving. My deal with Chris was that he would get paid once I passed through border control at the airport in Johannesburg. My cousin was supposed to sell my four-in-one printer for the money. I would call my cousin from the airport and she would give Chris $700 and keep the rest. The printer was worth a lot of money, especially in those days—people did not have them. My cousin agreed she would do this and Chris set everything in motion for me to go.

I passed through the airport in Johannesburg and stopped in Addis Ababa to change planes. Ethiopia Airlines had the cheapest fare to London. The deal was that when I got through Johannesburg my cousin would give Chris the money. I was in the airport in Addis Ababa when four men stopped me. They were very large and serious-looking men. I knew this would not be good news. Then said they had received a fax that told them I was attempting to board unlawfully. They asked me, "What is your nationality?" I told them I was South African.

■ ■ ■

They took me to the South African embassy. I went out to call my cousin. I said, "Did you give Chris the money?" She said no, she had not done this. She told me that this was because she was scared of Chris, but I knew her better. She was an older cousin, and I don't think she wanted me to go to the West.

By law, they should have detained me there in Addis

Ababa since really I was an Ethiopian citizen, but they let me go. They let me move about freely in Addis Ababa. Later, since I had said I was South African and they asked me so many questions about where I grew up and resided and what I told them convinced them that I was South African, and my surname and looks, which lead most to assume I am colored, it seems, did its magic so they put me on a plane back to South Africa, where I was in detention.

When I got there, I called my cousin. I had a nice denim jacket with me and I sold it for 50 cents just to make that phone call. I was back in jail again. Finally I called a lawyer, Chris. It was $150 to leave the jail. We had done business together. My friend had made money promoting musicians on tour and used my printing business to make the flyers. She collected a little bit of money from all of my friends, from everyone to bail me out. I had set everyone up with computers, so people knew me. I was very involved in the community, very well known.

Finally I was staying with Salaam and then I rented a home next to my church in Yeoville. I rented an office not far from there. I started working there and when I made some money, I bought a nice car, a BMW 3CS. It was my first real car. I had a girlfriend, Candice.

■ ■ ■

She was white South African. Her father had a business nearby. We were very happy together, and she gave me her cross necklace as a sign of her love for me. I treated her very well, of course, but her father did not approve of Candice having a relationship with a black man. We were very open and public about our love. Everyone knew about us.

One day I found he had sold his business and left, taking Candice with him. It was very hard to accept this, but it did not surprise me, since I knew the racial history of South Africa. Everyone does. It's just the way things were, and they have not changed that much for many people. I did not love Candice the way I had loved Billie—it was just a bit of fun, really—but I was upset to lose her like that, and for such an ugly reason.

I was doing very well in my business cleaning up and reformatting computers, and then installing Windows and MS Office. I also got a lot of mobile phones. This was 2002–2003. I became quite popular for this business, because everyone needed it. I was a local computer kingpin. Everyone used my business.

There were always people who would not pay me, though, because I was a black man. That's the way things can be in South Africa. Even other black people would disrespect someone who is black. I learned to use a white man to negotiate sometimes. They would do business with him and think that he had done the work. His name was Jack.

He ran the local pawnshop. People would pay him and leave their computers with him to fix, and I would do the work. Because Jack was white, he would get paid more reliably. I would give him a cut. It was frustrating not to get the respect I should get for doing the work, but on some level it was business, and I found a way to work around obstacles. That's the way I operate.

If there is something in the way, even if it is wrong, you can't always change it. I work around it, and the deal gets done. I make money. Life goes on. I can be practical like that. Jack was my middleman. Because he's white, people thought he fixed things but it was me.

I did business with all kinds of people in downtown Johannesburg: South Africans, Nigerians, Mozambicans, Angolans, Zimbabweans, Indians. One day I was doing business with a Nigerian businessman. He comes in with six laptops—he wants me to reformat them, load Windows, the usual. I get a knock at the door. It's the military police. They have big guns. The whole street is shut down. It's a big operation. They are after the organized crime ringleader for the theft of the six laptops. They arrested me and they arrested the Nigerian man who brought them in, Fefe. I said, "I don't know him. It was somebody else."

It seemed like the wise thing to do was to keep my head down and stay out of trouble. The authorities told me that I would get bail. I was remanded for further investigation. It was a big organized crime investigation. I waited for two weeks in jail. They sent me to the correctional center in Johannesburg. Fefe's driver came to visit me there. Fefe had gone to Lagos, but he paid for a lawyer for me, a famous lawyer. If you saw any of the recent over-age of the Oscar Pistorius trial, you saw my lawyer on TV talking about the case. He is a prominent lawyer in Johannesburg, very connected.

"You'll be fine," he said.

I left my phone with the driver and stayed in prison. I had 1,000 rand put into the prison commissary. I was in for six months in detention.

My lawyer was not always reliable. A lot of my friends in the local Ethiopian community started going to him and asking what was going on. He did not always show up for court. Finally I needed 1,500 rand ($150) for legal fees. Salaam organized the money. Later on when I saw that her list showed how little some people gave, I was upset, especially seeing the money Billie contributed, 20 rand ($2). This was heartbreaking. I had done so much for some of them but when I needed them to get out of jail, they gave me very little; as a result I had to cut ties with my community!

My lawyer said to me, "You are a smart person. I don't want to see you get involved with any more shady Nigerians."

I started working with the lawyer, doing business with him, bringing him clients. He gave me 25% when I brought in new business. He also set me up to do undercover work with the police.

There was a big undercover operation about to go down, a sting to root out corruption in the police force. There was a white ex-police officer on the west side that everyone was scared of. He was very powerful. He was taking drugs that had been stored as evidence and selling them in the white community.

The police came to me and asked me to pretend to buy drugs. I agreed to do it. It was a very tense situation. Once the deal went through, the police came in and arrested the white officer. I did it, but I never wanted to do it again. They called me and asked me to do more, but it was too tense a situation. It made me very, very nervous. I took the SIM card from my phone and threw it away and disappeared.

I started a new business as a negotiator, property broker, and angel investor. I was doing a lot of different kinds of business. I became a broker, a fixer. I helped my cousin, for example. She needed help trying to start a company. Even though she had treated me so badly, I still helped her, because she was family, and I knew that underneath it all she meant well. I always help people when I can. I believe people deserve chances in life. And besides, if her business were doing well, she would not have to bother me so much!

I ended up getting a property to manage. It was well located but also under control of criminals and in a very dangerous location. The landlord was not getting any money from the tenants. They were not paying. I rented it out from the landlord to sublease it. The tenants were Portuguese, Nigerian, Pakistani, and Indian. Everyone was frightened because of the neighborhood, including my cousin. The owner knew I was someone who would take a risk, and he gave me the sublease without asking for a deposit.

As the lessee, all of the tenants became my tenants. I took the lease for 65,000 rand and then went about cleaning up the building, restoring security and services, and collecting rent from the tenants. I knew that the building was undervalued for its location. Properly maintained and secure, it was worth a lot more. I increased rents 25%.

The tenants were not unhappy about this, though, because I did a lot of work to clean up the building. I cleaned up the parking lot. The tenants had thought I would evict them and bring in other Ethiopians. When they saw I cleaned it up and wanted them to stay, they were very happy. The parking lot, newly improved, brought in more money. It was a good business.

Around this time, I created this personality for myself, Derick. They all called me Derick. I had a made a life for myself in South Africa. I looked like a South African black person. It felt right that I should have a South African name.

I offered all the old tenants a lease. I also took key money, usually around 200,000 rand. I negotiated. The whole building rented out easily. I gave very generous terms. I could have used intimidation but I did not. I compromised with them. I wanted a relationship with them. In business you have to respect the other person. You can make money but you should not take too much.

I started making good money.

I decided to go to Ethiopia to stay for a short time. I was concerned about my mother's health. I promised myself and all my friends and associates that I would come back in five years. I went to Dilla, where my family was, that same small dusty town I had grown up in. It was on that trip that I met Maya, who would later become my wife and the mother to my daughter and son.

■ ■ ■

Before that trip, I had brought my mother and my younger sister Konjit to Johannesburg, mostly because of my mother's health. I took her to the Gordon Medical Institution

Research Centre, a very upmarket medical center where Nelson Mandela got his treatment.

She had been ill for many years, ever since the surgery she had when I was born. I wanted her to have the best of care. People come from all over the world to Johannesburg because of the high standards of medical care there. There are many facilities, opportunities, and expert, cutting-edge doctors in Johannesburg. This level of care is not available in Ethiopia. So I brought my mother there, and my sister with her, and took my mother to many places to see what we could learn.

Her medical troubles began when I was born. My name, Tariku, means story. We began our story together then. We never really learned what was wrong with her, but it was clear that whatever bothered her was alleviated when someone cared for her. You could give her a mint or a small candy and tell her it was medicine, and she would say afterward that it had worked and that she felt better.

Around the time when my mother came, I rented a small cottage in Johannesburg and stayed there with my mother and sister. The owner of the cottage was Edwin Cameron. He is chief justice in the Constitutional Court. I moved to that neighborhood because it was near the University of Johannesburg. I always valued education, and as much as I had a strong inclination and head for business, I wanted an education, too. So when my businesses started making money I enrolled at the university to study information technology and rented the cottage from Edward.

■ ■ ■

Most of the time Edwin stayed in his home in Bloemfontein, near Cape Town, but he came out to the cottage, especially when he was friendly with his tenants. He has helped a lot of people this way, I think, and I was one of them. He took me under his wing and offered mentorship and guidance. He was a generous man, someone who was very successful and smart, and I looked up to him as a role model: he guided me. He believed in education, too, and he believed in me.

He said, "Why are you going to do IT? You should study law or international relations."

It was because of him that I changed my course of study to international relations. Edwin is the kind of person who helps others and guides them. I don't know how I was so blessed to end up in his house. This is why I say angels were looking out for me.

Edwin is a trustee of Wits University. The official name is University of the Witwatersrand, Johannesburg, but everyone calls it Wits. It is the most prestigious university in South Africa. It has a long and grand history. Edwin is very important in the university, and he encouraged me very much in my studies. In addition to this, we shared a cat. He had two cats at his house. One was black and one had stripes. I was very lonely at that time and the cat was my best friend. She was special. One day she had an accident—I think she got into a fight. I took her to the clinic. She was there for one week. I was so worried. She needed surgery. After that I decided to get a bigger house. Later Edwin called to tell me she had been hit by a car and did not survive. I mourned for a week.

CHAPTER FOUR:

Arriving on a Bigger Stage: Transnational Businesses and a Historic ForEx License

AFTER I MOVED to the bigger house, I decided I wanted to make another trip to Ethiopia. I was driving from Addis Ababa to Dilla, and I spent a few nights in Awassa, a resort city. There were a lot of foreigners, NGO workers, and I stopped for dinner in a little café. This was the night I would meet Maya, who would later become my wife. She was sitting right there in the cafe. She turned out to be a friend of a good friend of mine. I got her number and started calling her. She was very smart and was soon to graduate from university in Awassa with a BA in journalism and literature.

After her graduation, I invited her to visit me in Johannesburg, but her family insisted we marry first. We had a beautiful ceremony in Addis Ababa, with many friends including Alfred, the economic attaché to the

South African embassy in Addis Ababa. He would later prove to be an important contact when I went on to work with the embassy. Alfred helped Maya get her visa to come to Johannesburg.

At this point I bought a big car, a statement car, a C55 AMG, black, 2006. I should have bought a Range Rover or a Ferrari. Most guys like a C class Benz, but the AMG is different, like a sports car.

■ ■ ■

I also decided to buy a house. We were living the dream, so I wanted the dream house to go with it. I bought a house with a big swimming pool, an elegant bar, a state-of-the-art entertainment center, and a library. I had two dogs, because that is something I thought every dream house should have—two dogs. We had a big garden.

I had a little cottage for the dogs. I called one of them Mugabe but I can't recall what I called the other one. My wife, now ex-wife, did not want the dogs coming into the house. She never liked the dogs. I wanted to have kids then but she did not. She had one vision but I had a different one. Her mother got involved and things would become very tense.

Around this time, I bought another property in Cresta, the main business area, from which to run my business,

Africa Holdings. At that time I was ready to go corporate. I set up a company and called it Africa Holdings. I set up a beautiful boardroom and reception centers, opening onto four offices. It was a big place, about 12,000 square feet.

At this point another woman came into my life. Her name was Miriam. She was part French and part Ethiopian and older than me, 36 to my 23 years. She had a very famous boyfriend—I cannot tell you who—but she wanted me. It was then that Maya told me she was pregnant. I wanted very badly to be a father, and it only seemed right for me to cut ties with Miriam. I was very direct with her and asked her not to contact me again. I hope I was not too harsh with her, but it was important to me to focus on my family. My daughter Elinor would soon be born.

■ ■ ■

Africa Holdings was the overarching parent company, but inside it I had, and continue to have, many ventures. One of my companies is called Abyssinia Business & Property and is a commercial property management company. During this time I especially focused on bringing my expertise in tech together with my understanding of the corporate world and the needs of businesses to save money when contracting a company for employee travel.

I started a business travel agency. I was an agent for kiosk.com and was keen to get business with Phoenix Technology in Canada. I went to Toronto to make a presentation at Phoenix of my online booking agency. I had other tech projects I was working on, too: Smart Reply and Voice Blast. Because my wife's father was in the travel industry, I already had an entrée into that industry and could see how it worked. I wanted to set up my travel business to target companies as my customers, to give them a more efficient and less expensive option for their internal use.

I was having a lot of success as an entrepreneur but I knew how things worked in South Africa. It has been over twenty years since the end of apartheid and even today I know I don't get the same treatment I would if I were a white CEO. Also, I knew that the white people who were there had the education to talk to my target customers. It was not what I might prefer, but when you are targeting the 1% for your clientele, you have to make them feel at home and send sales people and corporate representatives who look like them. It was similar to what I did when I used the pawnbroker for my computer business.

■ ■ ■

I would have a white face for my company, but I did the work. I designed the products, I studied the market, I built the business, and I made the money. This was not always easy. At one point I discovered that one of my marketers was not doing her job. She was supposed to give a presentation to BP, to their chief marketing officer, to show them how we could help them cut their travel costs. She did not do it. She presented someone else's product instead. I found out and I realized I would have to do this myself. It did not go well, and we lost business. I also found that white men sometimes did not want to work for me. Their egos would get in the way. I offered good incentives, cars, money, but they don't want to do it.

I was living the American dream. The American dream has been exported! I had an Audi A6, a beautiful car, and I bought a VW Kombi. But my wife did not want to drive the Kombi, the family car I bought hoping to have children I could to transport from school to home.

I closed a few deals, with BP and with Anglo-American. Thompson-Reuters called me. They wanted to buy me out. They were the competition. I told them their product was rubbish. I was disrupting the corporate travel industry, bringing in something new and better. I was able to tell prospective clients, "You can save 40% of your internal travel costs."

The world financial crash of 2008 was good for me

because I was there when companies needed to economize. I showed them how they would save money and I got their contracts. I had back-to-back meetings set up. I was a local business star. I was interviewed about my business insights for a one-hour television program called *Lunchbox*.

■ ■ ■

As the company grew, servicing the contracts became a problem. The call center needed more support. There was also a lot of credit card fraud then, which made it difficult to earn people's trust. People were wary of using credit cards online. I was the new kid on the block and I had to develop people's trust in my company and my brand. I did a big presentation in front of an important German company and they liked it.

At this point my business was a bit stuck—it was becoming difficult to win more customers. I decided to target end users, to compete with companies like Expedia. At this point, I had a problem with Google, because I was aggregating data from airlines and hotels. They blocked my company from their online ads. If I had played it differently, they might have bought the company. I was smart enough that I was disrupting technologies and Google noticed. I had their attention.

Still, I could see that my corporate business was not

doing as well as I would have liked. I bought a property from a company that was in debt 2 million rand to the city of Johannesburg. That property would later become the site and center of many dramatic events.

It would nearly cost me my life.

In 2009, Maya and I had a holiday in the coastal city of Durban. Along the beach there was a new development called uShaka Marine World, an all-inclusive resort with some of the largest and most up-to-date aquarium facilities in the world. Indeed, it is the largest aquarium in the southern hemisphere. It also hosts an oceanographic research institute. It's a very impressive vacation spot, favored by families, stylish young couples, seasoned vacationers, and companies using it for corporate events.

There are restaurants, water rides, and interesting attractions and events. After thoroughly enjoying our stay there, Maya and I decided to take an apartment on the beach. With our combined experience in the travel industry, it seemed like a good place to spend some time and build a new business. I already had a travel business in Johannesburg, and I decided to open another office there in uShaka. At this point we had three offices. I asked around and learned that AmEx had had a foreign exchange office there, but it closed.

A foreign exchange, or ForEx, seemed like a natural direction in which to grow my existing travel services, and it seemed to me that one was needed in Durban, especially in the very popular resort area of uShaka. The process of obtaining the ForEx license would prove to be very lengthy and difficult. Never in South Africa had a ForEx license ever been given to a foreign national, and it was very unusual for a black person to apply for one.

The Reserve Bank of South Africa was the official body that would approve or reject the license, and unusually, the South African Reserve Bank is not a government entity but is one of four reserve banks in the world to remain in private hands. Powerful Afrikaner bankers control it, and although there is a board of government-appointed officials that includes black South Africans, this board serves only as nominal figureheads. The true power and control of the bank rests with the old Afrikaner banking interests. These were the people who would spend a full year investigating me and whose approval I would have to win to be granted a ForEx license.

■ ■ ■

When I first started my application, the officers of the Reserve Bank were discouraging. Either they did not think I would pass the scrutiny of the investigation, or they did not want me to try. I think it took them some time to be accustomed to the idea that I could be a good candidate for a ForEx license. However, I was persistent, patient, methodical, and very hopeful.

I knew that my business dealings were all completely legitimate and I had confidence that they would soon be assured of this. When they would remind me that no foreign national had ever been granted a ForEx license in the history of South Africa, I would cheerfully and firmly remind them that though I held an Ethiopian passport I nevertheless had been for many years a legal resident of South Africa. Already I had worked to build several successful businesses by myself from the ground up. I had contributed to the business community and I had strong ties there to well-known people, all legitimate and respected members of the local community. I was friendly with and known to high-ranking lawyers and judges.

I knew that it was unusual for a black person to have this status and to try to gain access to the financial services, but I was confident that once they knew me, they would approve my license.

There were several requirements I had to fulfill in order to obtain the ForEx license. First, I had to open an office in Durban, which I did. I also needed to employ a compliance officer, which I did. I attended a seminar on the financial services industry, where I met a banking executive and consultant named Craig. I engaged him to act as a consultant on my application. He agreed to work for me, but I think he was later surprised when I was actually granted the license.

It was a tremendous honor and a historic occasion when it happened. I received the "love letter" from the Reserve Bank board telling me that I would be granted the license in 2009. I call it a love letter because it felt that way to me—I pursued something passionately and I was accepted. It filled my heart with joy just like a romance. I had seen a vision. I had pursued it carefully, honestly, and hopefully.

My love was returned! It meant a good deal to me to have these particular doors to the corridors of power in the financial industry, and I hoped that the global financial industry would open to me. Unlike others there, I did not have a degree, though I had studied at the best university in South Africa. I was not born into the world of banking and finance. I had worked hard and proven myself. I was and remain very proud of this achievement.

PART II

A Businessman's Vision
Puts His Very Life on the Line

CHAPTER FIVE:

Real Estate Development or Gang War?

IT WAS IN early 2006 that I began to make arrangements to buy a property in central Johannesburg. I had had my eye on this property for some time—a disused and abandoned petrol station very well located in the center of the city of Johannesburg, now used as a headquarters and storage space for a large taxi concern. It was 20,000 square feet and had a tremendous amount of potential.

Up until the end of apartheid, the petrol station had been operated by a business, Dual Investments, owned by white Jewish people. When apartheid ended in 1994, like a lot of other whites they fled Johannesburg, abandoning their business out of fear of what would happen next. And, like a lot of properties in Johannesburg, the now abandoned petrol station was taken over by others who wanted to use the property or keep it for themselves.

In this case, it was the Pretoria Taxi Association, a

very well-connected organization with ties to the ANC (African National Congress), the leading government party. The Pretoria Taxi Association ran taxi vans from Johannesburg largely on fixed routes back and forth to Pretoria, ferrying domestic staff that lived in in the poorer city center to tony homes owned by rich whites in the capital. They were managed and controlled by Zulus, the largest black indigenous ethnic group in South Africa, and the company itself was said to be a source of funding for the ANC.

Many of them had come from the ANC's military wing. As such, they were well connected in local politics and tremendously powerful. They had used the service station to quickly fill their tanks when the owners abandoned the property. It amounted to a kind of hijacking. I knew that they had taken over the property without purchasing it and that it would be difficult for me to gain control of it, but just how difficult, and how dangerous that might be, I was yet to find out.

Through a business associate of mine, a Zulu man named Elvis who leased an office in my suite, I learned that Dual Investments held the deed to the property, and that the city of Johannesburg had a tax lien against it for 2 million rand. In 2006, I met with a lawyer for Dual Investments, who said the company wanted nothing to do with the property anymore. The implication was that the owners did not want to upset the Taxi Association, for they were known to be dangerous people willing to resort to brutal and extralegal means to get what they wanted. Legally of course the property could not be transferred while there was an outstanding lien. The lawyer said that if I paid the city the 2 million rand and a small fee to the owners of 250,000 rand—ostensibly his own legal fees for the transfer—I could have the property.

The Taxi Association had in the years since 1994 accumulated a set of falsified papers including essentially everything but the title and the deed, showing that they now controlled or even owned the property. I went to them and opened negotiations, bringing Elvis with me. I thought it would be helpful if I had a Zulu on my team at the negotiating table. I suggested we form a company together and allow the property to pass into the hands of that company.

■ ■ ■

Since I was financing the entire transfer at a cost of 2,250,000 rand, I would take 80% and they could have 20%. They agreed. Dual Investments contracted with us to sell us the property at a future time under those conditions.

At this point I realized I had to perform due diligence

on the property before I could take it on. I also needed the Taxi Association to move temporarily so that I could do improvements on the property. The Taxi Association had not understood that they would be required to move. When they found out, they refused.

By then word had gotten out that I had contracted to buy the property under those terms—sharing the ownership with the Taxi Association, paying 250,000 rand to the lawyer, and 2 million to the city for back debt. Just as the Taxi Association began to sour on our deal over the question of vacating the property, my sister's husband's best friend, Solomon, heard of the deal. Solomon tried to step in and take it over. He went behind my back to the Taxi Association and offered the same amount of money. This happens a lot in business, but I did not like being squeezed out. The Taxi Association accepted and took his 250,000 rand with the understanding that they would repay the city over time.

At this point I started to see how dangerous they could actually be. Bruce, the lawyer for Dual Investments, had his office near one of the Taxi Association's satellite locations. With their reputation for brutality and their easy mobility, Bruce was anxious for his physical safety and the security of his office.

■ ■ ■

I wanted to pull out of the deal, to cede my 80% but Bruce said that Dual Investments would only do the deal if I were involved. He felt vulnerable to the kinds of strong-arm tactics he knew them to use. At the same time, the Taxi Association thought that Bruce was corrupt.

The lack of mutual trust further eroded relationships. Dual Investments could not sign over the title until the 2 million rand was paid.

In 2009, the city of Johannesburg issued a judgment of default.

I realized that there was a disused petrol station there that had never been properly decommissioned and that they were parking cars, dozens and dozens of cars, over a petrol tank, which had not been serviced or inspected for over 15 years. This, in the center of the city of Johannesburg. It was a huge hazard. I called the city. Immediately they dispatched heavily armed police and a South African defense force to evict the taxi operation. Television, radio, and newspaper reporters swarmed the area, which was sealed off by the police. Crowds gathered on the perimeter to stare. The cars were swiftly removed.

A couple of weeks went by, and then a court order came in. The taxi people were connected to the mayor, and the court order prevented me from taking possession of the property I owned. They were able to get in and remove the petrol tank. They broke into my offices and smashed things. Two assassins came after me.

I sent my family home to Ethiopia for their own safety. I closed the office for security reasons and I went to join my family in Ethiopia. I bribed the assassins to get them on my side, and worked to set up negotiations with the taxi people.

I called the city again to let the health and safety commission know that the people moving the tank were not professionals. They had no training or licensing in safety when it came to a handling a petrol tank or other hazardous materials. They were just laborers. It was still a very dangerous situation. I went to court and got an order to stop the work. At this point, the taxi people were willing to meet and negotiate. I told them that if they paid up, they could run their business there.

I built a beautiful shopping center over it. It cost me 48 million rand to build but it's worth 200 million rand now. It brings in $50,000 every month.

CHAPTER SIX:

A Foray into International Diplomacy

IN 2007, while growing my businesses in South Africa, I put an advertisement in a newspaper in Addis Ababa offering to help Ethiopians learn to do business in South Africa. At this point Africa Holdings operated a coal mine, a brick manufacturing plant, and (under the umbrella of Abyssinia Properties) had many real estate investments. I got a call from the South African embassy in Addis Ababa. They had seen my ad, and they also wanted to help Ethiopian people do business in South Africa.

Specifically, the South African embassy had a project funded by USAID, which counts among its areas of concentration economic growth and trade. The money had been granted to Fintrac, a large NGO that ordinarily works with USAID on agriculture and, perhaps because of this disjuncture, the project had landed back in the lap of the South African embassy. The project sat at the South African embassy in Addis Ababa, untouched, from 2002 to 2006. After I placed my ad, the embassy suggested that I bring the project to fruition. They wanted me to accompany a delegation of business and government leaders chosen by the Ethiopian Bureau of Standards to learn South African business practices.

As an Ethiopian by birth who had built a personal business empire in South Africa and beyond, I was well placed to know what the Ethiopian business leaders and government officials on the delegation would benefit most from seeing.

I included tours of such South African institutions as the South African Stock Exchange, the Department of Trade and Industry, the Department of Agriculture, the Department of Commerce, and the Bureau of Standards. I made contact with each of these institutions to arrange the visits. This would be a very high-profile tour with high-level leaders and everything had to be just right.

I first obtained a letter from the Ethiopian Department of Foreign Affairs granting me permission to submit a proposal. I next obtained a letter from Fintrac that recognized me as working on their behalf. It was important that I keep the South African embassy in the loop at every turn. I also worked with Ambassador Melese, the Ethiopian ambassador to South Africa, largely through the economic attaché, Abiye, who had been in that position for many years.

Ethiopian Foreign Affairs faxed the letters to the South African embassy. I then sent my proposal to USAID and they in turn advised the embassy that the funds were approved for the trip. Included in the delegation were many ministers coming from different government offices. They would expect a reception befitting their ministerial status.

I was additionally well prepared to do this work because of my studies in international relations at Wits, as well as my regular social interaction in Addis Ababa with people in the diplomatic corps and NGO workers and, to a lesser extent, in Johannesburg. The result was that I got the job done beautifully.

■ ■ ■

But before I could do that, the Ethiopian Embassy in South Africa became threatened. They did not want USAID to release the funds to me. They wanted the money themselves. They sent a letter to the Foreign Affairs office in South Africa stating that I was falsely operating as a government representative and accusing me of treason. Ambassador Melese himself called me and threatened that I would be charged with treason and thrown in jail. But the Foreign Affairs officers from both the South African government and the Ethiopian government reassured me that they liked the job I was doing. They asked me to please continue so that the trip would happen.

The trip was by all accounts a rousing success. Twelve delegates came to Johannesburg. They went to the embassy, where I had arranged that there would be appropriate gifts for them according to protocol. They took me to dinner afterward and lauded me for my efforts. The Ethiopian embassy had to apologize. They were embarrassed about how they had treated me when I did such good work. Abiye, the economic attaché, was pulled out of his position and called back to Ethiopia. I was offered a job with the Ethiopian government as a liaison with the World Bank, but I declined.

CHAPTER SEVEN:

Recruited into Politics, a Defender of Human Rights

IN 2008, after my daughter Elinor was born, I went on a bit of a road trip through Africa. I bought an Isuzu Trooper, an import from the US by a US diplomat as I was told by the dealer, who gave me a good price, loaded with camping gear and basic necessities. I drove from Johannesburg to Dilla, taking a route through Cape Town, Mozambique, Malawi, and Kenya to Ethiopia.

I wanted to visit Egypt, but I was stopped at the Eritrean border. On my way I passed through Tanzania as well. While I was there I heard about 250 Ethiopian men who were arrested and in prison in Dar es Salaam for illegal entry, just like I had been years before. They had been found crossing the border illegally in the back of a truck. I knew what jail would be like for them. They would not know the language. They would be uncomfortable, cold, underfed, forced to labor. I was very upset by this and went immediately to the prison, where I was able to bring them some things and visit with them. They were greatly cheered to have a visitor.

Having made something of myself in the years since I was jailed under much the same circumstances—also for not having papers—I called the Ethiopian embassy in South Africa, because there was no Ethiopian embassy in Tanzania. They were already working to get the men out. I offered to help by getting them a bus or even a plane but the government insisted that it was their job, not mine, to get them out.

■ ■ ■

I was very upset about this, thinking of those men in the prison. I drove back to Ethiopia, my heart heavy with thoughts of them, and went to the Foreign Affairs office to plead with them to allow me to help, but they would not allow it. I have thought so much about those prisoners. It is a cause very close to my heart.

It was in a similar public-spirited vein that I later received into my home the world-renowned Ethiopian jurist, opposition candidate, and former prisoner of conscience Birtukan Mideksa.

A member of the judiciary, Birtukan was appointed

as a high court judge. She became interested in political reform and became quite active as a member of an opposition party, the Coalition for Unity and Democracy (CUD), which in the 2005 election won more than one-third of the seats in parliament, a very impressive result that allowed them to claim victory. On the evening of the polling day, Minister Meles Zenawi announced on television that though the opposition had won in Addis Ababa and taken all the seats on the city council, the government had taken the majority in all four regions outside the capital and therefore had the right to form a government. In the same speech Zenawi further reminded the military that they were accountable to the government, backing his statements with a reminder of the might he commanded. He effectively shut the opposition out before the official results could be tallied.

Many people had hoped this election would lead Ethiopia to more democratic, multiparty rule. The opposition had won Addis Ababa in a landslide. In the weeks and months following Meles' announcement, a sense of outrage filled the capital. Massive crowds gathered in the city, taking to the streets to protest the government takeover.

The military took violent repressive action and fired into the crowd, killing (a report later found) 193 people. The judge who authored the report fled Ethiopia after it was released, fearing reprisals from Meles' regime. For protesting the rigged election and the effective seizure of the government, the entire central committee of the CUD opposition party was immediately arrested along with 1,000 followers.

Thirty leaders were sentenced to life in prison, including Birtukan, and in total some 80 people received lengthy sentences, including some journalists. They were charged with treasonous acts intended to overthrow the government of Ethiopia. Meanwhile, there were new elections for some 30 seats for which the results had been contested by the opposition. With the opposition CUD leadership all behind bars, the government handily won these seats.

Eighteen months later, after much international pressure the opposition leaders were granted a conditional pardon that restored their freedom and all their rights. The condition in question was an apology to the government for their role in the opposition. The apology was released through the media.

In 2008, after her release, Birtukan, already known in international circles as a brave progressive leader and prisoner of conscience, was invited to Sweden to address the national parliament in Stockholm. In her speech she publicly denied having apologized or requested a pardon from the Ethiopian government. It was a very risky statement and she received much media attention for it.

■ ■ ■

It was around this time in 2008 that mutual friends began to suggest that I should meet Birtukan. My prominence in the expat Ethiopian community in South Africa was growing, largely due to my success in business and my good social connections. It was just the year before that I had organized the USAID-funded delegation of business and government officials to great success. They see me as bold, unafraid to be different, a leader in my community with the potential to do much more.

I very much admired Birtukan's bravery and out-spokenness. Like me, she was young to be in the public eye, only in her early 30s. I said I would be proud to meet her. Other friends warned me, saying that if I did that the government would be after me. The atmosphere of fear was understandable given the violence and brazenness of the government's backlash against the opposition.

We met at Kaldi's, a local chain of coffee shops serving the kind of high-quality coffee that is to be expected in Ethiopia, the land from which coffee origi-nated. She brought a friend with her, Assefa—a guy from the embassy. When I saw Birtukan, she had a deep unease about her. She seemed shaken, restless. She was very pale and looked like she has not rested. She was paranoid, look-ing around her. I could imagine the things she experienced in prison. Very likely she was being followed wherever she went.

At one point I suggested to her that we go to the Djibouti border. It was St. Gabriel Day, a religious holiday that happens near Christmastime that we celebrate in Ethiopia. I asked Birtukan if she wanted to go with me to the church services.

■ ■ ■

There is a beautiful church near the Djibouti border and they would be having services that day. But her mind, sadly, was not on the religious festival's celebration.

It was on political intrigue.

"Do you mean to smuggle me over the border?" she asked.

I think she really believed that we had made this plan for her to get her out of the country. She had had some very bad experiences because of her brave stance in opposition to the Ethiopian government, and her ordeal was not over yet. I was proud to meet her but very concerned about her. You have to understand: Birtukan was very likely tortured in prison. The prisons there are notoriously brutal and she was there as an enemy of the state.

Two days later, on December 28, she was rearrested. The government claimed that the statements she made in Stockholm regarding the apology violated the terms of her release, and jailed her to serve out the rest of her life sentence.

Having seen her just days before her arrest, my heart was full for her. I left my car in Addis Ababa and flew to South Africa. I wanted very badly to help her. I want to know whom she knows. She has a very young daughter. I was talking to my friends in the government, telling them that they were wrong to do this. But my stay in Ethiopia for the Christmas holidays was over and I returned to South Africa.

■ ■ ■

At this point the former Ethiopian defense minister, Siye Abraha, contacted me. Siye was a very well-known national politician. He had been one of the leaders of the Tigrayan People's Liberation Front (TPLF), a party that had held power for many years, and after that a founding member of the Ethiopian People's Revolutionary Democratic Front, the party that was then and still is ruling the government. He had served as a government minister under Meles Zenawi. But then he joined the opposition. He was jailed and many years before he had appeared in Birtukan's court, and she freed him. After that, he joined her party. All of Siye's colleagues turned their backs on him for that.

No one would meet with him or return his calls.

So Siye summoned me back to Ethiopia to meet in person. He had heard that I wanted to help Birtukan, and her child especially. He knew me by reputation, as an Ethiopian businessman who had made a successful life for himself in South Africa, first, but also because of my work with the consulate to bring the delegation to Johannesburg.

I think he was interested to hear that a young person of some standing who had stayed out of the political fray in the past was bravely coming forward even in the face of the violent repression that had taken place under Meles. I was honored to have been invited by him and readily accepted. He took very good care of me while I was there out of concern for my safety. He sent a car to the airport to pick me up and welcomed me to his home to eat at his table.

■ ■ ■

He told me that he was shocked that a man of my age who could be out partying was showing such determination and courage. He said that he admired me for getting involved and showing concern about Birtukan, her young daughter now without her mother, and Birtukan's aging mother, who now cared for the child while Birtukan was incarcerated. He threw a big party for me and made sure I had a driver while I was there.

At one point while we were talking, Siye seemed very interested in something I had just said and stopped the conversation.

"Tariku," he asked, "have you ever thought about standing as a candidate?"

I was shocked and flattered that a man such as him, who had had such a long and illustrious career in politics, would suggest this for me. He had not only extended his friendship and hospitality, but he was also inviting me into his vision of a better Ethiopia. Here was someone who sacrificed for his ideals, even serving time in prison, and he thought that I could help to make those ideals come to pass for our country. I was very moved by the suggestion.

He asked me about my life and my business, and I told him some of my story. He thought about it, and he said to me that all of my experience was top notch and the things I had done in my life would serve me well, but if I wanted to be a candidate and help Ethiopia, I really should have a university degree. We talked about it extensively, what I should study, where I should go, what would best benefit me. I was very honored to have his advice. He was another angel acting in my life to guide me. I took it all in carefully and went back to South Africa ready to make some plans. At this point, I decided to study for an MBA.

It was while I was studying for the MBA in South Africa that at long last Birtukan was released. I shed tears of joy when I heard the news. Many people had worked very hard to convince the government to release her. In particular, the Swedes were terribly upset that she had been imprisoned again. There is a long history of Swedish involvement in Ethiopia, going back at least 150 years.

The Swedes and the Ethiopians have a special relationship, which was why Birtukan had been invited to come speak to the Swedish parliament after she was released the first time. The Swedes keep a careful interest in a lot of African nations, and Ethiopia is one in particular.

There were a series of international incidents turning on this political crisis. As a result of reporting about Ethiopian politics, two Swedish journalists were arrested in Addis Ababa and jailed. After the Swedes made a formal complaint, the Ethiopian government severed diplomatic ties, calling their ambassador back from Stockholm and expelling the Swedish ambassador from Addis Ababa. Nevertheless, the Swedes felt some responsibility for Birtukan, I think, because she had given the speech that got her into trouble at their parliament.

Finally, she was free! I invited her to come to stay at my home in South Africa. Everyone thinks this is strange. Why would Birtukan go to South Africa? At first she had some trouble getting her visa, but eventually it came through and she could come. When she arrived, Birtukan was with another woman, whom she introduced as a journalist, but I did not believe it. I think the woman might have been a spy to watch her for the Ethiopian government.

■ ■ ■

Not long after Birtukan arrived in Johannesburg, I was summoned to the Ethiopian consulate. Birtukan was even more nervous and paranoid than after her first imprisonment. I think she faced many difficult things in the prison. She advised me not to go and to refuse the meeting. I got upset with her about that. I disagreed.

"That is not my way," I told her. "I think it is important to talk to people, to meet with them, and to let them know who you are. Otherwise, how can anything be accomplished?"

She disagreed vehemently with me. She was very frightened, and I think she thought they would arrest me and interrogate me.

I decided that I must go. At the very least, I was curious about what they wanted. I had had experiences with the embassy before, and I knew some of the people who worked there so I was not afraid. When I arrived at the embassy, there was a beautiful dinner waiting, with a nice bottle of wine. Hibur, a political advisor to the consulate, greeted me.

Hibur was very connected in Ethiopian politics, and he had friends in Prime Minister Meles Zenawi's office. Hibur, Meles, and Siye had all worked together with the ruling party, the TPLF. Like the others, Hibur also did not acknowledge Siye since Siye had fallen out with the party. Hibur and some of his advisors welcomed me to the embassy and we sat and dined together. They were worried about Birtukan, they told me. I think they wanted to try to woo her through me but I knew that it was far too soon for Birtukan, and besides, Birtukan would not meet with them. Indeed, Birtukan did not even want me to meet with them.

■ ■ ■

I did not like what the opposition did. They had no record of running a government at any level. After the 2005 elections, they had won all the seats in the Addis Ababa city council and yet they refused to take them. They refused to take their seats in parliament. They wanted everything at one time, not the small amount that they had in front of them, so they refused it. Now they will never have that opportunity again. I believe that people should be willing to prove themselves. They should have run the city for five years to show everyone that they could do that and then run again. I did not like that decision.

Birtukan and I started having tension between us. I said to her that if I went into politics, I would expect that it would take me 15 years to become president of Ethiopia, not just 5. She said to me, with your way, that is not going to happen. The opposition started to say that I was on the side of the government. That was not true. We just had different methods.

Birtukan and the journalist stayed with me for twenty-one days. She wanted to stay longer and asked me if she could, but given how the visit had gone, I did not think it would be healthy for us, for our friendship, for her to stay longer than that. I said that three weeks was enough. At that point she already had plans to go to the US, where she would later accept a fellowship from Harvard University to study human rights in the law school.

I thought that she was turning her back on Ethiopia and on the future of the opposition. I thought she should have gone back to Ethiopia and convened a meeting of everyone who could work to change things, including if possible people in the sitting government.

■ ■ ■

Instead, Birtukan went immediately to the US to study, without doing anything in Ethiopia first. It shows an attitude that is typical in politics. She was not willing to take on the responsibility to lead people; instead she passed that responsibility onto others and expected that when she returned from Boston, people would still be behind her. I knew that her plan to go to the US would restore her spirit so she could enter politics later, but I still disagreed with the tactic.

After she left, I remained in South Africa and became interested in local politics there. It had started back in 2008 when I developed a product called Voiceblast, which I had presented in Toronto. It had been very well received. It allowed a campaign—most likely a political campaign, but anyone could use it—to blast out voice messages to thousands of people at an instant.

I came to know Dr. Mathews Phosa, a prominent member of the ANC who had established the first black-owned law firm in South Africa in the 1980s. In 1985 he was exiled, then later invited back in the 1990s to help lead the negotiations that ended apartheid and began to create a democratic system in its place.

I made a presentation to Dr. Phosa of my Voiceblast technology and they were very impressed, but ultimately they gave the contract to an American company. They liked me, however, and suggested that I consider applying to be a member of the ANC. Even though I was not a citizen of South Africa, I was a resident in good standing. I was eligible to join the ANC and even stand as a candidate, but I would not be able to vote. They sent me to Randburg to make the application.

■ ■ ■

It took one year for the membership to come through. They were eager for me to run as a candidate. I received my membership card and I did a presentation to apply to stand for election. The deployed me to run as a city councilor in Zandspruit, around Cosmo City. It was a very important part of town with lots of interesting things happening there. The woman who had held the seat before for the ANC, Maureen, was an old woman, and white. I know it sounds strange to think about, but there are white people in the ANC. It is not a segregated party.

Her son, Greg, was a sitting MP for Cape Town, but he wanted Maureen's seat on the city council when she retired. This is a little strange, too, because you would think an MP would have a higher position than a city councilor. It was because there are millions of dollars' worth of projects happening in that part of the city, and there was a lot of money to be made for a well-connected politician, I am sure.

There were development interests in the area who wanted someone in there who they knew would do business with them, so they brought Greg back from Cape Town to oppose me. Greg is a white guy with a lot of name recognition but for me it was just a start in politics. Greg and I ran against each other in the primary, and it was a very tense and heated election.

■ ■ ■

I did a lot of work to build support in the community. I got loudspeakers, too, to promote my name on the streets. It was a strange but exciting thing—to go out on the street and hear my name over loudspeakers. I was running some initiatives in community development, too, so people in the area knew me. Finally the primary day came.

The first thing that happened was that Greg called the police station in the district and told them that there would be violence in the polling place. It was a very white area and the police there were clearly racist. Since Greg is white—even though he is an ANC candidate—they did what he said. They started asking people to show identification when they came to vote. All the young people were kept out of the polling place. They were out on the street, beginning to protest. I tried to calm them down.

Finally the vote came, but only the members in the

room could vote. Sixty-five voting members were needed for a quorum. When the votes were counted, I got 28, and he got 32. So there was no quorum, and no candidate was chosen. At that point an older woman came out, someone supporting Greg, and started making a speech, saying "We know that there are foreigners among us who are trying to destabilize our election process."

I knew what that meant. By foreigners, she meant me, because I am Ethiopian by birth. I didn't want to become too angry or cause a scene after being targeted in this way, so I decided it was best if I left.

After this happened, there were many young people out in the streets protesting. The media came and covered the unrest. There were people chanting and shouting, and young people burning tires. They blocked the streets, angry about the rigged election, and outraged that the police, who were told not to admit the younger people who were supporting me, had kept them out of the polling place.

■ ■ ■

Greg had come up from Cape Town expecting to take his mother's job when she retired. He did not think he would face strong opposition in his own party, but he did, in me. He had to fight hard to win, and eventually he did. I was not prepared to fight dirty. I still want to make a contribution to politics, but I cannot do it in a system that blocks young people from having their rightful say at the polling place.

It was at this time that I finally finished the Johannesburg Shopping Center. I worked to build it phase by phase, planning each part of it myself with the help of engineers and architects. I invested a lot of time and money in that property. I had to sell my car and even my ForEx business to finance it. Initially I thought I would sell the property, but because of the difficulty with the Taxi Association, that became impossible.

Even with the success of the shopping center, I reached a turning point. I had had to drop out of my MBA program to attend to my business. My marriage was crumbling, and my wife had decided to go back to Ethiopia. It looked to me like she would not be coming back. I decided that I had to focus on my studies, and that it would be a good idea to study in Europe or the US.

First I applied to Harvard Business School. They wrote to me and told me that I was already doing well without their degree, and that I probably did not need it, while other students did. They wished me good luck in my future prospects. I applied to Stanford University, too. They wrote and told me that they had gotten thousands of applications, and they did not have a seat for me. I applied to the London School of Economics but that also did not work out. Finally, while researching business schools on the Internet, I read about the Swiss Business School SBS in Zurich. I decided to apply.

I was interviewed in South Africa and eventually I had a telephone call from the dean, Dr. Wolf. He expressed surprise that I wanted to come study there, saying that I did not need it. I told Dr. Wolf that I needed the qualification, and that not having a university qualification was proving to be a roadblock for me in my career.

I had someone helping me, Advocate Kobus, who was representing me legally in business interests. Kobus advised me to take a break from Johannesburg and go to Zurich if that's what I wanted to do, to be a full-time MBA student. I thought that that was what I had to do, because I had so many responsibilities holding my attention in Johannesburg, keeping me from pursuing my studies. I had already begun and left school three times due to pressing business concerns. He said, "Go ahead and get away from here for a while." I put some people in my company in charge of my affairs to manage things for me while I was gone.

I told my wife that if she wanted, she could go back to Ethiopia with the kids, or she could stay here in my house. I told her I was selling the big American dream-style house, which she hated, after all, and buying a house in a guarded complex in Johannesburg. That was what she had wanted in the first place, so she decided to stay while I went off to Zurich. It was exciting to think of the new beginnings that awaited me there, the things I would do with my new degree, and the connections I would make that would allow me to begin doing business on an even larger scale.

CHAPTER EIGHT:

*A Ticket to the World of Global Finance
and Life of Mystery*

ARRIVING IN ZURICH was very exciting for me. I had already made a great success in business for myself, first in Addis Ababa, then in Johannesburg, and here I was arriving in Switzerland to study global finance. My ForEx license had been only the beginning. I would soon, with the help of the degree, be operating on an even greater scale.

My first apartment in Zurich was a tiny place. It was such a shock to me, coming from Africa, to see the very neat, economical interiors of an old European city. Dean Wolf, who had interviewed me over the telephone, was surprised that I would want to study for an MBA.

"But, Tariku, you are already doing so well! We shall certainly be pleased to have you if you choose to come."

He and his wife welcomed us with a lavish party at a

well-appointed Zurich restaurant. The exquisite food, sub-dued yet luxurious décor, and the expectant faces of the business school community let me and other new students know that a degree from this university would open doors to a new world of influence and success in business.

At that party I must have made quite an impression on Dean Wolf's wife. She was a delightful person, and though there was certainly nothing sexual or inappropriate in our feeling for one another, we got on well and, following the party, often socialize together, sometimes with her hus-band and other friends and sometimes just the two of us.

We recognized something special in one another, seeing another person who valued success in business through hard work and shrewd thinking, and also felt a kinship in our love for refinement and conviviality when the business day was done. We both shared a taste for fine dining, and Zurich had many worthwhile options that suited this interest.

We spoke freely on a number of topics, and always had a good time. It became clear soon after my arrival that I fit in well with the high-flying jet set at the school and in the higher echelons of the local business community, and I would soon be invited to take part in a very high-level deal that could be worth billions of dollars.

In the meantime, I found the transition to life there to be quite smooth, despite the difficulties foreign students and travelers often face when adjusting to a new city in a country that speaks a new language. Most people who are visiting struggle to get a visa to stay for a longer period in Switzerland. The process can drag on for a long time, and the Swiss are very meticulous about the paperwork. All of the communications are in German, and when I was communicating with the Swiss embassy in Johannesburg, the officer there kept insisting that I had to hire a German translator.

Of course, this is how they refer business to their friends. I did all the translation work myself with Google Translate and some other computer based translation software and was always very efficient with my replies.

■ ■ ■

The officer I dealt with chided me for not hiring a translator because he wanted me to do it his way, but he could not argue with the quality of my results, though I felt that he had in some small way turned against me. Perhaps that would add to the difficulties I would later experience, though I had no way of knowing this at the time. I was very successful in the process.

It only took me about one week to get my visa, and I received a type B visa, the highest one, which would allow me to work and to study. People were impressed that I could get the type B and were perhaps even a little surprised, but I knew that I had handled it well, and I think the reference from Dean Wolf opened the door to a new life in Switzerland beyond that of an ordinary graduate student and paved the way to success on a larger world stage.

My fellow students in the MBA program came from all over: Germany, London, the United States, and Spain, among other places, but they elected me to represent our class. I felt very proud of this, and I knew it was because I was making so many positive connections. I felt confident that the MBA was already introducing me to a caliber of businessperson that would challenge me to do the sort of work that was truly suitable to my capacities and would expand my skills even more. I felt alive, excited to begin my studies, and to look at the world with a renewed sense of possibility in the company of the best the world's business community had to offer.

On the first day, I met Stephan, who came from Denmark, and would become a fast friend. I also met Roger, who claimed to work for a car dealer and was a white Zimbabwean. Because of our shared background in Africa, we understood one another well.

He knew what kind of life I had made for myself as a successful businessman in Johannesburg, and like the Dean's wife, he recognized in me another person who appreciated quality. Soon after arriving, I wanted to buy a car so that I could get around in my new city.

Roger helped me a good deal, because my visa had not yet come through. We took the train together one hour out of the city and with his assistance I purchased a BMW Z4, a beautiful car that would demonstrate my place in the world. Roger also helped me to get license plates since the visa was still pending.

I began to really enjoy my success, both in Zurich and in South Africa, as I basked in the recognition of my peers, and came alive with all the possibilities that lay before me. After helping me to make the transaction to buy my Z4, Roger invited me to an exclusive VIP party at the Dolder Grand, a very upscale hotel popular with the most glamorous people in Zurich. This was just the first of many such nights I would have. I became very socially active.

I was on fire.

I began to date a Swiss woman named Desiree, whom I met on the social network Badoo. Since I am very good at computers and very social, I meet a lot of people this way. Desiree and I dated for a while and saw one another exclusively until we began to drift apart. It was not a difficult breakup. We had had a lot of fun among the fashionable young set in Zurich and we were each ready to move on. During this time, I decided that my kids should come to stay in Zurich and attend school there. My wife and I were legally still married, but both pursuing other relationships. We knew that our time together as romantic life partners was behind us, though we still shared a complete devotion to our children.

My success in South Africa began to be celebrated locally at this time. I was nominated for and then granted a very prestigious award in Johannesburg for business. I returned in late October to accept the award and enjoyed spending time in my home business community, where I received a lot of attention for pursuing my master's in Europe.

I was traveling from Zurich to South Africa, back and forth, for business in one place and for my MBA studies in the other. At the airport passport control they began to recognize me and understood why I would be traveling so much, so it was fortunate that I had such an excellent visa.

I would meet South Africans in Zurich who would ask me when I was coming back to settle in Johannesburg, I think a bit nervous that I would not return. They offered me properties to buy in Cape Town. By leaving Johannesburg to go to Zurich, I had raised my profile at home significantly.

Even though I flourished in all of this intense activity and international travel, something happened that nearly brought it to an end. My shopping center, which I designed and built over the disused petrol station that had been under control of the Taxi Association, suffered a series of power shortages. This created a crisis situation for my tenants at a critical point in the project's development.

I returned to South Africa and found that the situation was complex and would require more of my time than I could devote were I to continue as a full-time MBA student. I telephoned my friend and ally Dean Wolf to give him my regretful news. He suggested that I come for dinner with him and his wife at one of our favorite local restaurants, a quiet but elegant place with a good steak and a top-notch wine menu where we could talk further.

I went with a strong sense of a sad mission to convince him that necessity was driving me from the school, for the problems besetting my business in Johannesburg could not be handled even by my trusted attorney Advocate Kobus, and my presence was needed. What the Dean offered me that night at dinner buoyed my spirits and renewed my joy. I could study in the Flexi-MBA program and still earn the same degree but only attend class three times per month as a part-time student. This would allow me to spend more of my time in Johannesburg and remain active in the management of my business affairs there.

Once the dean saw how pleased and relieved I was to be able to stay, our conversation became much lighter and my diminished mood lifted. Then the dean told me that he had some very exciting plans for a business deal and that if I were going to stay, he hoped to interest me in participating in the deal. My ears perked up and my senses came alive, as they always do when I sense that an exciting business opportunity is about to cross my path.

You might say that I have the heart and the senses of a lion, noble in its bearing, attuned to the sounds and smells of his environment, and able to pounce with great ferocity to make his killing. What the dean suggested next made my eyes blaze with the thrill of the hunt. The dean had a connection to Stadler Railway Corporation, a Swiss company that wanted to develop trains for sale and use in South Africa. He sought my help in securing the financing for the deal on the South African end.

■ ■ ■

This was potentially worth $10 billion US if we were successful. In that moment at the dinner table, it became clear to me that all this time the dean was gauging my worth for a larger purpose, and I expressed my sincere interest in and enthusiasm for taking part in this truly high-level deal. Dean Wolf told me that we would have to set up a company in Switzerland to handle this aspect and that I would have to go back and forth to Johannesburg to broker the particulars as we went forward. He already had a network of people working on different aspects in the nearby city of Zug, and he put me in touch with an adviser there, Dr. Martens.

I made contact with Dr. Martens and we made a plan to meet very soon. For a variety of reasons having to do with the local business environment, he strongly advised that I base my new company in Zug. In order to do that, I must also move to Zug so that my address was in that city.

I went to the immigration office in Zug and they told me that in order to register there as a foreign national, I would first have to deregister in Zurich, which I did. Then I rented a large house in Unterägeri, a sleepy little mountain town far from the glamorous bustling social life I had been living in Zurich. It is a beautiful little town and I found the quiet and privacy to be a soothing change. I expected that it would give me some peace to think and to approach a deal of this magnitude with calm and fortitude. The lease I got was for one year, and my kids decided to join me in Switzerland to attend school and live there so long as I did. They applied and were granted visas. I expected them to arrive on December 10.

On December 6, a snowy early-winter night, I sat alone in my home warming myself by the fire. It had been a long week of making plans for the Stadler deal, as well as plans for my kids to arrive from Johannesburg in just a few days' time.

Their rooms had to be ready and mentally I prepared

myself for the joyful, noisy day-to-day of a home with two young children in it, rather than the solitude I had found 50 kilometers from the city of Zurich.

At around nine o'clock I received a message on Badoo, my preferred social networking and dating site. It was from a woman called MC, a beautiful and playful professional model of Norwegian descent. We had flirted mildly before, exchanging some messages, and now she wanted to meet over dinner that same night. She was insistent about the timing.

"Derick, why won't you come? I have reserved the best table," she cajoled (though it was just a text message in the app, it was as if I could hear her voice already), as she named a very stylish new restaurant that had gotten a lot of good advance buzz, and that I wanted badly to try. She knew how to get to me already, it seemed. "We will have such fun," she continued. "I can tell you are just the kind of person I like. What is stopping you and what can I do to change your mind?"

I explained that it was already late, and the snow was falling steadily and thick. My house was in the mountains, so the drive could be dangerous. It was 50 kilometers to Zurich. It would take an hour, maybe more under those weather conditions. I had planned to stay in, prepare a simple meal, and rise early to work on my many projects again the next day.

Still, her attempt to convince me brought a smile to my lips.

■ ■ ■

"I want very much for us to meet, MC. Surely you must know that! I agree we will get on famously. That is a certainty! I like your energy very much. You have nearly convinced me to go out in the cold. Here is the thing: I would have another long drive back through the mountains with even more snow on the roads after our dinner. I prefer to be able to relax when we do finally meet. I would not want to worry about having to drive, and especially not late at night during a snowstorm. I suppose I could get a hotel room, but honestly I prefer not to do that."

I left it up to her to extend an offer if she was so inclined, and she did.

"Nonsense. You'll come to mine after dinner. You can garage the car near the restaurant and forget about driving until tomorrow. It's settled, then, yes? See you at ten."

She wasn't entirely clear what she meant when she offered to put me up at her place for the night, but I had a good idea of what she had in mind. Anyway, she was gorgeous, a professional model, and gave off a fun, flirtatious vibe. I dressed in my best suit for a night on the town and a fresh shirt, and drove carefully through the mountains into the city. I found a garage to take the Ford Mustang and arrived at the restaurant at 10:02.

The restaurant she chose specializes in fresh seafood in simple preparations to showcase the quality of the fish. The lighting is very modern, in different colors, and the food is plated a bit dramatically. The music was electronic, but with an easy, low-key feel. After I checked my coat and came in from the cold, I noticed that she already had champagne on the table.

"I admire your foresight," I said to her, smiling, as I bent to kiss her cheek. "That looks very refreshing."

We enjoyed sashimi and ceviche appetizers and then moved on to lobster. The conversation flowed as easily as the wine, and I felt relaxed and comfortable. We didn't have too much more in common than our love of living well and enjoying a fabulous evening out, but I didn't need much more to enjoy myself with MC.

After the coffee was served, we had not had enough of our night on the town. She suggested we go to Amber, an upmarket lounge. I had been to Amber once or twice already with Roger and I knew that it was expensive but worth every penny. I have worked very hard to make a success of myself and one of my true pleasures is to enjoy a delicious cocktail in the perfect setting in a world-class city. We were having such a good time together and I wasn't ready for the night to end. So how could I say no?

We took a taxi to the lounge and I took our coats to the coat check while MC went to find a table. It was approaching midnight and the club was filling up with stylish people wanting to see and be seen, and we were no different. I hope I don't flatter myself too much when I say that we made a striking pair, and I was looking forward to the hum and buzz of the fashionable lounge, as well as the pleasurable hum and buzz of my inner engines, fueled by a couple exquisite cocktails and the pleasure of MC's company.

When I emerged from the coat check to find her, however, it was clear that something had changed. I immediately saw that MC has not gotten a table yet. Rather, she was there on the stairs with another woman, who, like her, was tall, slender, and striking. Suddenly, a shockwave ran through me. I was transfixed by this second woman, her poise, her hauteur, her beauty.

■ ■ ■

I felt deep inside myself with great certainty that I am about to meet the one woman above all whom I am most drawn to in all the world. It is as though she is already my wife, as if our souls have known one another for a thousand years.

I reach out and steady myself against the handrail

and hope that MC has not noticed that the entire world has changed completely for me. After all, she was the woman who asked me to join her for dinner. I felt everything around us slipping away, as if only the two of us were present: me and this mysterious woman on the stairs.

I tried to talk some sense into myself, to maintain my composure, and bring myself back to earth. *Whatever happens after the date is over, for tonight,* I reminded myself, *I came here with MC and I have to respect that.* I came with MC and I will leave with MC. She must not have any inkling that another thought has crossed my mind.

All of my upbringing and all the values I held in high esteem as I strove toward excellence in the world demanded without question that I remain with MC and continue to focus my attention on her. To turn to this other woman, this mysterious creature that had already changed my life, would dishonor MC and would dishonor me in turn. I tried to hold steadfast to this principle. This proved to be quite difficult.

The woman on the stairs graciously and coolly invites us to come join her at her table. She turns to her right, gesturing broadly with her arm, pointing us toward a prime spot in the back of the room. She takes an extra moment to regard me directly.

■ ■ ■

There is no shyness in her. While at most a fraction of a second passes, it feels like minutes as I meet her gaze. In that brief moment, it is as if no one else is there. It is as if the world around us freezes but we continue on alone.

And in a split second that moment passes and we are each interacting with those around us again, the woman turning to MC and laughing lightly at a clever remark. The whole encounter is uncanny. The two women are similar in looks and build, with pale blond hair, bright blue eyes, and striking chiseled features.

Both women are undeniably beautiful and could grace the pages of any fashion magazine or runway. Except the woman on the stairs has a presence about her that I cannot describe. She is nothing short of magic. Even as I try to hide the effect she is having on me out of politeness, internally I am reeling as though finding myself suddenly on a cliff face, teetering at the very edge. I am certain, from a feeling deep within me, that she is my wife.

Before we go to the table she speaks to me. It seems as if hours have passed that night alone, and yet just a moment ago I encountered her for the first time.

"I'm Naomi," she says.

"Derick," I respond, meeting her powerful gaze with equal fervor. As we shake hands for the first time and a spark passes between us, I ask, "What do you do, Naomi?"

She eyes me with some interest. "I am a lawyer."

This pleases me: a connection. "I am a lawyer, too," I say. "Informally."

■ ■ ■

I am thinking of my time advising asylum seekers and writing their cases as well as my time working with attorneys in Johannesburg. I am not a lawyer, technically, but many times I was told I was a bit like one and that I was doing the work of a lawyer, so this seems fitting. It is the first thing we have in common, that we are both lawyers.

I learn that she is also a former Miss Switzerland and a professional model. I tell her about my business ventures, about my investing, and about my work toward an MBA in international finance. I am completely open and unguarded with her in a way that I rarely am when I first meet someone. She asked me who I was and I gave her real answers. I was looking into her I eyes and felt strongly that I had to. What would be the point of holding back, since clearly our souls have known one another over centuries? As I speak, she listens attentively.

There is much banter between the three of us: Naomi, MC, and me. The conversation is quite lively and Naomi and I match each other with our energy and confidence. They seem to be fighting over me. At first it is playful, but the energy between the two women heats up at a certain point and they exchange barbs.

They glare at each other with fire in their eyes. Naomi wants to dance with me, but I will not do that. I will not disrespect MC, whom I arrived with, and I know Naomi and I are connected in a way that goes well past this evening. I will wait. Naomi and MC continue to challenge each other. They start dancing together and then go to the restroom together. I am trying to put aside this spectacle because it is a little embarrassing.

■ ■ ■

I know that Naomi wants me, but it would be unfair to MC to respond in the way I want very badly to respond. They return from the restroom and the conversation continues. The two women dance together again, and then Naomi turns to MC and kisses her, right there in front of me, the person they were both really interested in, and in front of everyone.

I had never seen that before and I know in that moment that Naomi will do anything to have me. Such is her passion. She whispers in MC's ear, and MC declares that she is going home with Naomi, back to Naomi's apartment. I am very confused by this, but looking back now I see that they were both trying to win me, and that Naomi would stop at nothing. Angry and frustrated, I removed my car from the garage and drove back to Zug alone. They are shocked.

A week passed while I turned these events over in my mind and bided my time a little. I called David, a friend of MC and Naomi who was there that night and got Naomi's number. She agrees to meet me at the Hyatt Hotel in Zurich.

I greet her warmly and tell her, "I like what you did. You will do anything to get what you want."

We ordered wine and talked about business. I see a lot of synergy between her business plans and my past experience. Naomi wants to start a company, to be an online booking agent for model shoots that could be used by agencies and magazines to book models and photographers. As a former professional lawyer and model she knows the industry quite well.

■ ■ ■

Since I had mentioned at Amber that I had founded an online booking agency for travel she is very interested in working with me. She knows I will understand her business and I do, immediately. She clearly values my experience and my input. After discussing her plans and my own experience, we decide to do business together. At a certain point, she lights a cigarette. I ask her to stop smoking. It is bad for her health and she is someone I care about. She gets angry with me, very upset, and leaves me there at the Hyatt.

This is where things begin to get mysterious. A week or so later, I was at a party in Zug, in the middle of the night. The party is quite successful. The room hums with the conversation of elegant people and the clinking of glassware. It is in a cozy upmarket club, similar to Amber but on a smaller, more intimate scale.

I'm chilling out and having a good time. There is a woman there, very good looking, and like Naomi she is tall, slender, white, with blond hair and blue eyes. I don't see her face very well because of the lighting. She also owns a club and she knows everybody in this one, too, and is buying everybody drinks. She buys me a drink, too. Later, she walks in front of me and I get her number. She watches as I scroll through my phone, and flirting with me says, "You have so many friends." She is also studying for a PhD in law, just like Naomi.

She tells me her father is a kind of king. At the end of the night I tried to leave with her but the security in the club prevents it. Later, when I look her up on WhatsApp, her profile is Naomi. I get a shiver down my spine when I see the photo. They are the same person. I know it in my heart. I cannot say for sure because the club was dark, but you know that women can look very different if they change their makeup.

The same woman could appear to be a totally differ-ent person in a dark club with the right makeup. I cannot prove anything, but I know it in my heart to be true. If you have a lot of money and a lot of friends, if your family is powerful, you can be whoever you want.

Our lives are meant to be entangled. The threads of our fates, intertwined. Soon she will call me for a meeting and propose a business venture. But the proposal I have for her goes far deeper. It pulls me across continents and oceans in a storm of powerful forces coming together.

CHAPTER NINE:

Powerful People, Powerful Ideas, Powerful Love—
A Tempest of Possibility

NAOMI BEGINS to email me about her company, Fashion Factors International. She is developing an online booking engine for models and photographers. It will do many of the same things that my company, myteambooker.com, can. She asks me for another meeting, so I drive back early from a trip to Milan to see her. She doesn't reply to my messages.

On January 7th we meet, at an event put on by a very exclusive and elite group that I am a part of called InterNations.org. It is a group that has been very helpful to me in my international business traveling and frequent relocations. You meet only the best traveling and expat foreign nationals at their events, all over the world. They are very careful about whom they let in, and you cannot go unless someone who is a member invites you. It is very selective. I invited Naomi. I am sure that by offering her entrée into this very high-status international club I am showing her a tiny glimpse at the kind of life we could have together.

She brings a friend with her, Stefan. As usual Naomi and I have very intense energy together. We both have strong personalities, and we challenge each other continually in the conversation. The presence of her friend and of my friends in InterNation.org moderates and tempers this dynamic somewhat.

■ ■ ■

On this occasion, she brings up her company again, and she asks me to be an investor. She lays out a plan for the business and asks for $100,000, which makes sense because of all the things her company will need to do. Our conversation is intense, though, and at one point I ask Stefan to step away and give us space.

Later he leaves, fed up. When we are alone, I agree to make the investment. I tell her I will take on a partnership in her business. I go on to tell her I want to merge everything with her. I want to be partners with her in the business and also personally, in our lives. I let her know that I am willing to do both of those things.

I want her almost to marry me, but not really because

legally I can't yet do that. I can see her and what she wants in life. She was a Miss Switzerland finalist, she is a lawyer, and she is studying for two PhDs. I feel strongly, deep in my heart that I am what she is looking for. I can see where her life is going and I know that together we can do amazing things. We make sense together. We have so much in common. I can see a shared vision for us to have a life together, a very happy, successful, and fulfilling life. We have a very strong energy connection. I explain this. She says, "Stay away from me."

She gets on her bike and she flees. This is on January 10.

On January 15, I got a letter from the Swiss government immigration bureau telling me that I was in violation of my residency permit. The letter stated that I should not have relocated to Zug, nor should I be setting up a company, and that because I had violated the terms of the permit in this way, they were giving me 30 days to leave Switzerland.

The letter stated that I would also have an opportunity to respond to the order if I wished. I decided that it would be for the best if my wife and my two young children went to Johannesburg for the time being, while I myself moved back to Zurich to sort it out with the immigration office.

I thought back to the efforts I had put in prior to my arrival in Switzerland and recalled the antipathy of the Swiss immigration officer who insisted I hire a translator to prepare my documents. That officer had scoffed at my hard work to do my own translation.

This was a translation that I did by myself using Google Translate and other computer software, into a language that I did not know! It spoke to my abilities, and probably frustrated the officer and surprised him that I was able to do that, and so quickly at every turn.

Perhaps his obvious distaste for my choice to do things my own way—something that has always characterized my personal style and continues to contribute to my success— was now part of what was blocking my stay in Switzerland. I was concerned that this officer might handle any appeal I might file. It could not help my case if there were someone in the office against me, whether he was a high-ranking officer or even just a clerk.

I decided that the simplest thing would be just to leave Switzerland. I was getting irritated by difficulties I was having there. I had many parking tickets mounting up. The letter I received from the Swiss immigration bureau left a sour taste in my mouth. Where was the warm welcome that had greeted me when I first arrived in Zurich? I messaged with Naomi about it. She was surprised that I would give up so easily.

"Why don't you fight it?" she asked me. "You say you are a fighter. So get a lawyer and fight!"

She was right. Still, she stopped returning my messages and I began to get suspicious.

It started to dawn on me that Naomi could somehow be behind the letter, that as powerful and connected as she was, she might have some way of influencing the government in these matters. I had no way of knowing for sure, and with people so powerful it is difficult to know how they operate.

They move behind the scenes. Things are done based on a handshake after a quiet conversation. One telephone call from someone truly powerful can change the course of someone's life.

A call from such a powerful, connected person could keep an extremely capable, clever, and hardworking person from achieving his life goals, from finishing an MBA, from completing a $10 billion US deal.

Perhaps Naomi was not such a person just yet, but what about her family? What connections did they have?

Once I started to think about that, I started to see the world differently. It also made me concerned for my future relationship with Naomi. Did she have problems that were not clear to me from our earlier interactions but were beginning to show now? Was she playing with me? Why?

■ ■ ■

What wrong did I do to the Swiss government that they terminated my study permit abruptly? Is it a crime being an entrepreneur?

The more I thought about it, the more my suspicions I grew and wondered what was my crime. Had she used the networks to which she had access through her powerful connections and social position to have them send it or was she acting on behalf of the Swiss government?

It made so much sense and yet it made no sense at all. Here was a woman of power, depth, intelligence, and (need I add?) uncommon beauty. We were already at our first meeting locked in a dance that surely had spun through the centuries, in our souls.

Our conversation flowed, and we pushed each other to new peaks. It could not be anything but obvious to her that we should be together. What a success we would make! In the business world, on the glittering social scene of jet-setting global citizens!

To walk away from this—to flee in anger—was madness.

■ ■ ■

That madness would show itself further in the coming days. I have no way of proving these things, but I know them in my heart, like I know my own name, like I know my grandmother's face.

I left Zurich, for as surely as powerful forces and influential people beseeched me to stay, I am a gentle warrior. Too many things were happening to push me away. The parking tickets were a headache. The letter from the Swiss government told me that I was being watched and that I was unwelcome. I met the most magical woman, and yet she repulsed my genuine and well-intended overtures.

I was already planning to go to Munich for a holiday, and that made it easy to go. While I was driving through the Austria, high in the Alps, I began to receive messages from a Badoo account. I knew it was Naomi. It had to be Naomi. Otherwise, who was this person? It was the eeriest experience: every turn I made, every stop, she knew where I was. She knew all my movements.

At first I thought, this person is very clever. She can guess very well. Then I thought, she must really know this route. But after a time, it felt stranger and stranger, like she was there with me all along, watching me, coyly chuckling to herself at her clever game. She never said she was Naomi, but I knew it in my heart, as I would come to know the truth behind so many mysteries that would unfold.

Nevertheless, it felt eerie, uncanny, how well she knew my movements on that trip. We texted and texted all night, bantering sociably, telling stories of our personal lives, discussing family and children. She was very charmed by me, and I warmed once again to her buoyant and engaging personality.

Everything that had passed between us that was difficult or confusing seemed to fall away in those small intimacies of SMS, though it hovered there between us, an unanswered question. She was coaxing me to come back the next morning.

In Munich, at my hotel, I tried to convince a guy I met of how important this was, whatever it was that was happening between me and Naomi, between me and the mysterious woman who was messaging me on Badoo that night, for they were one and the same. He was not on my level. He was not seeing the whole of the universe as I felt I could see it. In my heart I was flying once again, messaging with her. The man in the hotel tried to calm me down. I must have looked quite mad, raving at him at the bar that night. She made me drive back to Zurich the next day, and so I did.

On January 19, I went to the Hyatt in Zurich to meet another woman, not Naomi, just someone I was casually involved with. I saw a woman there who could have been my wife's aunt. Her aunt was living in Germany, and though I had met her only once, I felt her eyes on me, judging me, following my every move.

I knew immediately that I must leave the Hyatt and not meet the woman. I went to my wife—my now ex-wife—and demanded a current picture of her aunt. She began to cry. She would not give it to me. I knew something else was wrong, once again, with my life in Zurich. Was it the Swiss government, blocking the growth of my business and career? Were they similarly motivated to prevent me from finishing my MBA?

Did she do it because she was confused, because she was not yet ready to trust me, because she had some underlying problem that made her behave erratically, or because she was acting on behalf of Swiss government, which forced her to push me away because they suspected I was a spy that had come to Switzerland?

I go back to South Africa, leaving my Mustang behind at the school for Roger to tend to. I meet a man in Johannesburg, Bernard. Bernard has a way of seeing into you. He taps into your mind. He is like a coach. I met him one night in Johannesburg when I was eating at Tony's Spaghetti restaurant in Northcliff. It is one of my favorite places to eat. I always go there, and everyone who knows me, knows that. Anyone who might be watching me would know that, too. I love Tony's Spaghetti.

Bernard is sitting near me, and he keeps trying to catch my eye. He wants to talk. We begin to talk and I tell him the story of my life in Zurich and why I am no longer there. Bernard is recording our conversation. He tells me he wants to write my story. He had been paid to be there by someone else, but by who is not clear.

He is talking to someone else from Zurich, and of course Naomi is in Zurich still, studying and setting up her business. Bernard convinces me to take a house in Johannesburg and he introduces me to a very stylish interior designer. The designer has an associate who is a former miss South Africa, and very beautiful, like Naomi. The two women work together on my house. I spend $40,000 US on furniture to make the house just right for my new life.

During the period of time while this is happening, I go on Facebook, and there is Naomi again. This time she is using someone else's Facebook account to talk to me. She does not use her own name but as always I know it is her. She asks me for airline tickets, so I send them. This happens three times, but three times she does not come. The third time I send them through Roger, my friend back in Zurich. The third time, I go to the airport to meet her. The former Miss South Africa tells me that she knows Naomi is coming. I wait at the airport for one hour but she does not come. I suspect that she knows about my friendship with the former Miss South Africa, and is confused by this and does not come for this reason.

I start sending Naomi direct messages, SMS messages, saying she has psychological problems, as I was eager to know the motive behind her actions. This upsets her, I think, because of what happens next. All along I thought she had sent Bernard to me and had sent other people to test me, to see if I was genuine and would truly take care of her.

I cooperated with them so that they would see that I had nothing to hide. But now, once again, she is pulling away and will not come to visit. Finally, Roger and I decide I must approach her with an incomparable gift. I have him sell my Mustang at a loss, for only half of what it's worth, so I can do this. I have a special Rolex watch made for her, and I send Roger as my emissary with the gift. The watch costs $8,000 and I give Roger another $4,000 for his services in helping me sell the car, procuring the gift, and delivering it to Naomi. He drives four hours each way to give her the gift. When he arrives with the watch, worth $8,000, she starts screaming. She threatens to call the police. But she takes the watch and she does not respond to me.

Around this time, in April, I get a call from my lawyer in Zurich, who says I could get a visa to return by applying through the normal channels. He suggests that I submit a business plan for the company I was setting up with the dean. So I do this. They like the business plan and I get the permit. I immediately send it to Naomi. I tell her, "I need your help with this. I will give you 49%." Naomi calls my lawyer and tells him that she will block my business permit. She tells him that I am stalking her. I cannot understand what she wants. I call the lawyer again, and this time I tell him to cancel all of my applications. Withdraw them all. I am not going back to Zurich now. He asks if I am serious and I tell him I am. I am getting tired of this bullshit.

I decided to set up a company in New York instead, and in October 2013, I come to New York to run the American side of Africa Holdings. Little did I know that as I planned to launch my business and my brand on a more global stage, mysterious forces would follow me still and thwart my every move.

Despite the difficulties that would follow, I would also move in glamorous circles, make contact with important people that would bear fruit, and begin down a path that would lead me eventually to the woman I would marry. Who would that dazzling woman be?

PART III

*The Making of
a Global Business Mogul*

CHAPTER TEN:

Intrigue and Mystery Follow Me to New York

WELL IN ADVANCE of my departure for New York, I started doing a research to find suitable accommodation on Airbnb. After signing up I managed to secure a comfortable apartment in the Wall Street area, which I expect will be very close to the financial world in which I am planning to work and build my business and will also offer easy access to the stylish centers of downtown Manhattan. The apartment I take is available for six months but will not open up until about ten days after I arrive. I will need a short-term accommodation for the interim period.

Strangely enough, I soon receive an email from an unknown person advising me to rent an apartment from a woman named Sahel, via Airbnb. She has a pleasing apartment, comfortably furnished with good light in the

West Village at 88 Greenwich Avenue. I decide to take the apartment.

I was invited to attend a special luncheon meeting at UN plaza by the secretary general of NEPAD, an arm for African union. I didn't know what the meeting all about but it was scheduled for the second day after my arrival in New York. I was overjoyed and excited to receive such high-level meeting invitation and could imagine the opportunities waiting for me in New York.

When I arrive in New York, I proceed immediately by luxury hired car to Sahel's apartment. I am not slightly tired from the flight and am mostly energized as I go over all of my plans in my head for launching myself in this exciting world capital.

The possibilities give me tingles.

Sahel is there at her apartment, waiting for me with her own luggage packed for a two-week stay in Boston. She tells me she is glad that I have arrived because she has to leave very soon to catch her plane. She lets me into the apartment, which is just as I expected, and I am very pleased. She is genial and kind but since she must dash to the airport to catch her own flight, I don't wish to delay her unnecessarily. I simply thank her kindly and accept the keys.

Since I'm a little worn from my long flight and hungry, I walk out with her, leaving my bags, and go in search of a restaurant for a light lunch and a celebratory glass of champagne to toast to my new start in New York. New York, at last: a global city at the highest echelon of international trade.

I wave and smile to Sahel as she gets into her taxi, and she waves back at me. At a nearby café, I choose a salade niçoise and call first for one glass of their finest champagne. My spirit warms with the small amount of alcohol and my heart bubbles up with the perfect French vintage as I consider my next steps and make plans to schedule meetings with important contacts. The greens in the salad are fresh and bright. The tuna is perfectly seared, vibrant, and rare in the center. I am very pleased. With a healthy lunch in my belly and a heart full of anticipation, I head back to Sahel's building to unpack and settle in.

At the front desk, I am surprised to find that the card key she has given me to pass to the elevators does not work, though she tested it before she left. The doorman sitting at the desk tells me that I cannot go in without Sahel.

A slight panic begins to descend on me. Behind those locked doors and upstairs are all my things. I paid for my lunch with some cash I had in my jacket. Even my wallet is behind that wall. Hiding my growing alarm, I argue a little with the doorman, but respectfully, because I know he holds my fate in his hands.

He will not budge. If I am Sahel's guest, he tells

me, then Sahel must admit me to her apartment. No exceptions will be made. This is the building management's policy. I look at my watch. By now her flight has taken off. I lean onto the counter to brace myself as the blood rushing in my head begins to thunder in my ears.

Here I am, alone in this city, with no one and no way to get to my things, not even to my wallet and passport; I had brought a few bills to the café for my lunch and nothing more. From the corner of my eye I see a police car just outside and for a brief moment I stop breathing and my head spins.

I flash back to the time I was taken to prison in Dar es Salaam from the hostel where I was staying. My things were beyond the front desk, the receptionist at the desk would not let me pass to my room, and the police came to take me to prison.

Without my passport and wallet I was no one to this New York doorman, and I would be no one to NYPD, I was sure of that. As well-dressed as I was in my fine handmade jacket, high-end designer jeans from Zurich's most fashionable shop, and Italian calfskin shoes, how did I know they would not just see me as a stranger and foreigner without papers, trying to go where he was not welcome?

Without anything on my person to prove that I had paid handsomely for my stay in this well-appointed apartment, would they believe me? Was I right to think that the police were there because of me, or was it just a coincidence? Perhaps the doorman could simply push a button and summon them silently.

Perhaps these officers were known to him or the management and would do their bidding for a fee. I was familiar with police and official corruption all over the world, and I had read that New York City was not always so different. So many fears and possibilities filled my head. The officers sat in their car in front of the building.

I thought I saw them glance my way, but I couldn't be sure. I decided it was better not to find out and did not press my case any further. I gathered my nerve, calmly thanked the doorman for his consideration, and asked with reserved politeness whether I might wait in the lobby for Sahel, given our misunderstanding.

He eyed me, and clearly appreciating my pleasant demeanor—I think he expected me to be more confrontational—he returned my outward gentility in the manner of someone trained to show outward courtesy to a refined class of guests and invited me to sit. I settled myself into the modern leather sofa, took a deep breath and sent an urgent text to Sahel conveying my distress at this new development and demanding her immediate return. Outside the police officers sat in their car and the sun continued to shine on a beautiful autumn day. While I waited for her call, the fate of my new life in this world-class city already in jeopardy, I practiced the meditative skills I had learned in the past, which had gotten me through many difficulties before.

When Sahel calls me, I plead with her to come back immediately. Initially she doesn't want to, but she can see what a terrible spot I am in. She is a good person, I think. I offer to pay for her ticket if she'll come back right away. She takes a deep breath and agrees to do it. With nowhere to go, I wait in the lobby until her taxi pulls up.

She is deeply apologetic, and I believe her when she says she had no idea this would be a problem. I will have to rent another space. She refunds my money. I spend one night at the Peninsula, treating myself to a bit of comfort, and then move to an apartment in Times Square that I find on Airbnb. The same ten days cost me $5,000, but I have to live somewhere.

When I get to the apartment in Times Square, it is stuffy. I can't breathe in the apartment. It has no light, very few windows. My phone doesn't work when I'm inside. Someone is jamming the signal, trying to intercept my communications.

They followed me, even though I have just rented this apartment, and already there is electronic surveillance in there. I need to calm down. This apartment will not be the sanctuary I need from which to launch my future success, but it is only for ten days and I am strong. I have survived many months in a terrible prison and worse. I am strong in my body and in my mind. I go to sleep, but mentally I have one eye open, watching out for danger, for traps, and for betrayal. In my stay in New York, there will be many who come after me. Because of my inner strength and calm, they will not win.

Finally it is time to start my lease. I leave my place in Times Square to go retrieve the keys from the real estate agent. He meets me in front of the building, at 20 Grand Street. But when he opens the door and enters the apartment, I see immediately that it is not the place I saw in the pictures.

It is not the same place at all. It is ugly and dark, menial, simple, not luxurious at all. Someone is messing with me and making things hard for me. I get very angry with the real estate agent. I am coming to the end of my patience with this. I don't know if the real estate company is involved, if someone is paying them, but I am sick of it. The agent calls the owner of the company and she comes over.

When I see her, she looks just like Naomi. I can't help but remark on it. The owner is very gracious, and we end up having lunch. We discuss my business and what has happened with Naomi. She tells me she can see what kind of person I am and that I have a lot of good things in my destiny.

I tell her that I am beginning to suspect that the Swiss government is involved. A sharp businessperson, she tells me she thinks I might have a PR problem in Switzerland and advises me to return. Why am I being showed the road to Switzerland?

After lunch, she shows me a much better apartment, far more suitable, in Executive Plaza, across from the Michelangelo Hotel in Times Square. It is not where I want to be exactly, but it is far better than the terrible one they were trying to pass off to me on Grand Street.

My mind is wondering about the scheduled meeting before I left South Africa at the UN with high-level officials, so I have to focus and settle my mind and withstand all this turmoil I faced upon my arrival in New York, the city never sleeps, the Big Apple. I'm hoping that I will have a slice of the apple.

■ ■ ■

I dressed in my best suit and carried some of the investment opportunities that I gathered in case I bumped into potential investors at this special meeting. I reached the meeting early in order to network and introduce myself. The meeting was on the 21st floor and you had a 360-degree breathtaking view of New York City. The Japanese ambassador to the UN approached and introduced himself to me and we both started admiring the breath-taking view by walking from one corner to another. He asked about South Africa and Africa in general and I shared that Africa is growing very fast and with so much opportunity. He invited me to visit Japan and meet investors who might wish to invest in Africa. Here now I see a bigger picture of what Africa Holdings can do and finally my vision coming to reality!

More people started coming to the meeting and the secretary general for NEPAD introduced himself to me, followed by the South African ambassador to the UN and the former Japanese ambassador to the UN. They all handed their business cards to me and were very excited but I had to control my emotions.

The special advisor to the secretary general of the UN came to me and offered me all his support. We all sat at the dining table and food and drinks were served with different cheese and champagne and wines. The former Japanese ambassador was very keen about my life and sat next to me. She was an older lady and noted on her business card that she was a professor who resided permanently in New York. The vision I laid for Africa Holdings had caught powerful people's attention! There were a few Americans in real estate development at the meeting as well who offered for support in whatsoever I needed!

■ ■ ■

I was asked to introduce myself and share my background, which I did briefly and went straight to the project I was holding, and it was a $300 million US project in the coastal city of Durban, and the former Japanese ambassador asked me to drop the document at her home, which was at her business card address.

The meeting was a door opener for greater opportunity that lay ahead and my head filled with positive energy and I couldn't wait to deliver the project I had and reconnect with powerful people who were able to open great opportunities.

It is around this time that things begin to turn darker and I start getting threatening messages and calls not to contact the former Japanese ambassador to the UN and I'm being unsettled in New York.

First I hear from Sahel. When she returned from her trip to Boston, she found herself locked out of her apartment. Her keycards no longer work for anything in the building. They have canceled her lease and kicked her out for renting on Airbnb.

I felt bad for her, and wanted to help her, since I was the person she rented to. I let her come and stay with me for about a week, maybe ten days, just a little while so she could get on her feet again because she had nowhere to go.

When she first arrives, everything is fine. She is a lovely person and keeps to herself, except sometimes in the evening when we have a cocktail together. After a few days, things don't feel quite right. I start to suspect that something is strange about her presence in my life.

First she rents me this apartment that I never get to stay in, and when I arrive, the police are there, watching. Supposedly she has flown away on a plane but quickly she comes back again to get me. It isn't normal for things to happen that way. Then she must stay with me—that is also very strange.

I let her come because it doesn't take a lot from me to be kind to her when she is having a difficult time, and I wouldn't want anything bad to happen to her because she rented her apartment to me. Still, I begin to notice that whenever I leave the apartment she is there and when I come home, she is also there. I keep a close eye on my personal items and I am sure they have been moved slightly, as if someone has looked at them or has been looking through my things.

When she talks on the phone, she closes the door, and she always keeps her phone with her. I never get a chance to see it, though I wonder who she is texting. All the time she is texting. After a time I think she is keeping track of my movements. She is friendly to me, but there is a distance there. I wonder what she wants. I wonder who has sent her.

She claims to be a former Iranian supermodel who runs successful modeling agent in Dubai and tells me that she has run away from the UAE government because of charges I don't understand. When I Googled her full name I found her father has successful business in Geneva, in line with what she told me.

I don't know if she is working for the Swiss government, but whoever it is must be very powerful. Once I begin to see this, I tell her I think she has stayed long enough. She nods and accepts that. Within two days she finds another place. If she is a spy, she is not a professional one, or she is not one to make trouble. I never see her again.

Nevertheless, I am glad when she goes. I cannot have someone I do not trust sharing such small quarters with me. My space must be a sanctuary so that my mind can be clear. I am here with a very important purpose, to launch my business on a global scale. I am finally in New York, a city that can accommodate my talents. Already I have been invited to exclusive parties and met many important people. I cannot have interference in my own home preventing me from fulfilling my powerful destiny.

Then I start getting threatening messages. I found a building in Times Square I thought would be attractive to lease and then sublease, but that deal also fell through because of interference. Nevertheless, I was determined to continue to forge new connections to build my brand on this new world stage. I fought hard against discouragement, and sought out relationships and opportunities wherever they presented themselves.

One night soon after I had begun negotiations on the deal, I went to a Meetup for successful businesspeople at the Empire Hotel, and the deal that had fallen through in Times Square came up in passing in conversation with a man I met. It was a friendly enough conversation when it began. He had studied business in school and was facing some challenges as he began his own company. This had been a primary life goal of his for many years.

As a successful entrepreneur, I knew I had much to offer him and greeted him warmly. The Times Square deal came up as an aside, but for some reason it upset him. His eyes narrowed, his brow furrowed, and his face darkened in an ugly snarl. He began shouting at me. He accused me of coming to New York to lie. He said I was there to bullshit Americans. He was quite angry and abusive. His breath was as sour as his words were poisonous. This was very shocking to me. Here we were in a refined, sociable business setting with smartly dressed and successful people all around us shaking hands, enjoying beautiful top-shelf cocktails, and generally forging alliances to support one another in their endeavors. Everyone was amiable, courteous, and open.

Indeed, I had just been offering the man my encouragement and advice from my many years of experience and struggle! I was terribly affronted and taken aback at his sudden turn in demeanor and felt myself physically recoiling from him.

As I did so, he shouted louder and gesticulated at me, chopping the air repeatedly with his hand in a motion that mimicked a machete coming down toward my head. I could see that he was trying to intimidate me and was terribly confused.

One of the leaders of the group that evening intervened, firmly stating he would not hesitate to ask anyone causing a disturbance to leave. At that point the man began to accuse me! I was terribly shocked and felt my face color at this depth of disrespect.

Luckily, there was a very attractive woman in a finely tailored suit who was watching. She had been making eye contact with me from across the room before the man introduced himself to me. She saw what was happening and she approached the leader to speak up for me.

"Excuse me, but I happened to see all of what has just happened. This gentleman has been nothing short of gracious this evening," she insisted, referring to me. She paused for just a moment to cast a cold eye at the angry man who had accosted me. It was clear the group leader knew her and he waited for someone else to speak. Still very flustered, I felt some of the weight of the anger come off of my chest.

Here was some justice at last, in the form of this kind woman. I gritted my teeth a little and made a decision to rise above this and demonstrate to my beautiful savior that indeed, my manners were much better than those of the shouting man.

Into the awkward silence I managed to insert, "I'm sure there has been some misunderstanding."

I hid my anger and pushed it further down in hopes that lighter, more positive feelings would arise so I could take some enjoyment from the evening.

The leader gave us a rather general warning and the man slunk away into a corner, muttering under his foul breath, to nurse his whiskey and glower. I took a breath and smiled at the woman who had stepped in. We introduced ourselves and began chatting.

Out of the corner of my eye I noticed that the shouting man had disappeared from the room. The woman was very welcoming but nevertheless the strange suddenness of this assault on my psyche made it very difficult to carry on. I accepted another drink from my new friend and listened to her plans to launch an app for legal services, to take my mind off of the incident. Nevertheless, the ugliness that had been visited upon me by this nasty stranger stuck with me like a bad taste in my mouth. Even the beautiful salmon canapés passed by the waiters did not tempt me. My good humor was destroyed. After inviting the woman to meet in the future to answer any questions she had about her startup, I gave her my warmest wishes for success, made my excuses, and returned to my apartment.

The click of the lock as I let myself into my apartment was solid and clear, reassuring to my spirit and tempering my racing heartbeat. I felt my blood pressure drop as I looked around and saw the apartment in perfect order. I felt the chaos of the world outside shrink. The noise, dirt, and constant assault on my senses and being that I felt outside in Times Square receded. The room was silent, clean, furnished in elegant simplicity. There was a light scent of lavender water from the fresh flowers the housekeeper had arranged while I was out that day. I took a deep breath. I felt protected here. Safe. It was my refuge from the storms that were swirling around me.

So many things happening to me one after another could not be a coincidence. Why had the man targeted me, after all?

As I thought back, I recalled that he had chosen to introduce himself to me. In my mind, I pictured the first few moments of our meeting. He saw me across the room, smiled—was it a knowing smile?—and strode toward me with his hand outstretched. At the time I took it to be a friendly gesture, for what else could it be? I did not wonder that he had chosen to speak to me first out all the others there because I knew I made a good impression in my hand-tailored jacket and Italian calfskin loafers. Not everyone is usually so smartly turned out.

I began to wonder whether he had some connection to the people who had interfered with the deal. I thought carefully. Everyone knows that Meetup profiles are publicly viewable, and of course I had used my full name so that my new business acquaintances would be able to get to know me as I really am. I have nothing to hide and much to be proud of. It would be incredibly simple for anyone who wished to threaten me to find me on that site and follow me to the event. My head swam as I began to consider this very real possibility. I made myself a cup of tea, put on some calming music, and resolved that I would put the matter out of my head and make tomorrow a better day. This is always my attitude, and it has served me well and helped me through in many adverse circumstances.

During those weeks in New York, I steeled my spirit against the tide of negativity that was flowing toward me, but when someone mistreats you over and over, it has an effect. When many things are done against you, over time, it can wear you down. It does not create a positive atmosphere for good connections or creative actions in enterprise.

Whenever you are building a global brand, there will

be people who work against you, but you still must be in a positive place so your mind can be clear. It is especially nefarious and clever, if you wish to wear someone down, to target that person at unexpected moments, when he feels happy or relaxed, when he thinks he is having some success.

Soon after the night that that man yelled at me, the deal for the building in Times Square fell through. As the time to sign the papers approached, I began to get intimidation from unknown persons. First my phone would ring and no one would be there when I answered. Telephone messages were left on my cell phone at first, then delivered by hand to my doorman.

The messages said I should back away from the deal. The later ones said, "It might be a good idea to leave New York." One even said I was wanted by the FBI. It was terribly menacing, and I was growing tired of the feeling that so much was against me. As much positivity as I put into my everyday life, the tension began to get to me.

At this point, I thought to myself, it has to be a government behind all of these things, because it is obvious that government resources have been used. It seemed clear to me that it had to be a government. Who else was capable of doing all these things in so many cities? It must be someone very powerful. A government seemed to be the only logical answer. It did not occur to me that Naomi was so powerful that she could command them.

In New York, so many things happened to me. There was Sahel's apartment, and later Sahel's arrival. There was the apartment that had the electronic surveillance of all of my actions. There was the man yelling at me in the Michelangelo Hotel, but here were also other such people. Living in Times Square was like running a daily gauntlet of assaults to my inner peace.

My mind could not function well in that environment. Men would bump into me on the street, jostle me, and shout at me. I had bruises from the force of the encounter. It was like a ballet that represented the hostility of the environment toward my aims of success and general happiness.

I would be walking along the street and, BAM! The thick flesh of a stranger, stale and rank with the lingering scent of a habitual smoker, would smack into me, disturbing the cleanliness of my body and the smoothness of my thoughts with a small act of force. And just as quickly that person would disappear.

Or sometimes as I passed, someone would begin shouting at me, nonsensical things, but in such a nasty way that the sense of threat hovered in the air.

As I saw how often this happened, I wondered if they knew where I lived, where I habitually took my breakfast, and where I went at night. Did they wait for me there?

Did they text each other to exchange information about my movements?

Who had sent them? More than once, the ones that would bump into me would rob me of something, like my wallet or my phone. When your phone is gone for an hour before you notice, many things can happen to violate your privacy. They could have access to many things.

My jacket was stolen from a table. It was the third time it happened. It happened in Zurich, too—my jacket was stolen. Then in New York, one night I went to a very glamorous, upscale club in Columbus Circle near the CNN building. It was an exclusive club called Stone, very difficult to get into, with only the most stylish people. I had decided that I needed a glamorous night on the town to improve my spirits. And even there my jacket was stolen.

The more things happened, the more certain I became that it was deliberate. It was not normal. I suspected something was going on from the beginning because I have the kind of mind that does not miss details and is quick to understand their meaning, but at this point I was certain. Whether it was Naomi's family, though, or the Swiss government, I do not yet know.

Then strange things happened when I used my laptop. I would type something with the keyboard and the cursor moved, but no words appeared. It ran terribly slow, with the simplest applications dragging on. The Internet was very spotty. There were cookies from sites I had never visited, and processes running that, as an expert IT person with a long history in the tech industry, I knew to be suspicious.

I came to understand that Naomi could see everything that I did. I remembered that I lent her my laptop before I left Zurich and I realized that she had hacked it. Even while I was making many important connections and being warmly welcomed into many exclusive parties, I could feel worn down. I was getting sick of everything negative that was happening to me.

At a certain point, it was enough. I decided that I would go back to Johannesburg when my lease was up at the end of October. I knew then that it would not be the end of my efforts to launch my companies and brand in the United States. There were too many exciting forces drawing me to the truly global business world in New York.

Still, I missed my family, and I had important business matters to attend to in Johannesburg. I made some appointments with some of the well-connected real estate agents for exclusive properties that I had met at posh Manhattan cocktail parties. I signed a lease beginning in January in a much more suitable location, far from Times Square and everything there that wore me down. When October ended, I bid farewell to New York for several weeks' rest from the intensity of my new project. I looked forward to recharging myself at home and reconnecting with my business in a more direct and hands-on fashion.

■ ■ ■

Even as I relaxed into my first-class seat on the way home to Johannesburg, I knew I would soon return to New York. This time, however, I would be armed with the wisdom of one who had already withstood the challenges of making a new start on such a grand world stage.

In my short stay in New York I had already made many well-placed connections across a range of interests. Among these were highly connected real estate brokers who catered to elite business people, especially the international set, who required only the finest accommodations and best addresses for New York homes, whether short- or long-term.

This included Rachel, a real estate agent of Nest Seekers International. Nick warmly introduced me (at a quiet, elegant cocktail party in a friend's Upper East Side penthouse) to Ryan, a million dollar listing agent who runs a reality TV show. He was very warm and friendly and assured me that he would have properties that would be suitable to someone of my tastes and needs.

CHAPTER ELEVEN:

A Venture Capitalist Seeks Investments

I SIGNED a lease that would begin two months later in January, for 88 Greenwich Avenue, incidentally the same building Sahel's apartment had been in. This time I would rent the penthouse. The intervening two months would be just enough time to return to South Africa and attend to my affairs there and to lay some plans for new business ventures. I assumed I would find attractive investments in Africa or Europe, but it was not long at all before my mind turned once again to the United States.

In building my business brand for the next stage of my career, it had become increasingly obvious to me that I had a compelling story to tell of my humble beginnings, my struggles in the face of great adversity, and my rise at a young age through the international business elite.

Many of my friends and associates in Zurich and later

in New York expressed curiosity when I told them of my roots in Ethiopia and astonishment as I shared the dramatic tale of my eventual emigration and success in business.

So many people had put their faith in me, looking over my shoulder and watching silently and giving me encouragement when I most needed it, and helped me to make my luck by giving me work or supporting my efforts. They saw good qualities in me even before I knew I had them, and the more I told these story of my life to my friends, the more I knew that I could repay these kindnesses by showing the world how the faith of good people can help lift a young heart and mind to work hard for success. I needed a writer to help me do this, so I set about searching for one.

I contacted Ron, a writer, investor, and business-branding expert located in Fort Lauderdale, after finding his page on the web. Our initial consultation went well. Much to my delight and surprise, I found in him a helper who appeared to share my vision. Even better than that, he convinced me after just a few conversations that he wanted nothing more than to help me realize my vision for success.

He tells me that I must immediately come to see him in Florida, where he lives, where he will broker for me a very promising business deal. I am impressed by the qualifications presented on his web page and the poise with which he presents himself. He is confident that the deals he wishes to present to me will be more than worth the long trip from South Africa to the US.

Further, he warms my heart with his invitation: I must stay, he insists, as his personal guest in his home. In just a few short days over the telephone, we have become trusted confidants and will soon become partners, we are sure, in some business venture or another. Ron has many to show me. It will be an exciting trip, an invigorating trip for someone who loves the art of the deal.

It is a long trip to Fort Lauderdale, Florida, from Johannesburg, connecting through JFK, but I am excited at last to meet Ron in person. He is also very pleased to meet me and comes to the airport to greet me and drive me back to his home. I am a little tired from the journey but overall I feel good. In an earlier part of his career, Ron worked for NYPD prior to starting his own business as a branding expert.

■ ■ ■

As a result of this, he has many connections to the military and law enforcement. He offers me his protection and guidance. He understands intuitively that I will need to be protected, without having to be told of all my woes and difficulties.

I wonder if there is some chatter in international law enforcement circles about the obstacles I am facing that makes him want to do this. At any rate, it does not matter: I am safe with him. We talk a little business after I arrive and then sit down to a lovely meal with his family. He tells me about some troubles he is having with the neighbors and I offer some suggestions from my years of experience working through tense negotiations as an informal lawyer and later in political affairs. He listens carefully and appreciates my advice.

The next day Ron and I fly together to San Juan, Puerto Rico, to meet his business partner.

In San Juan, the business partner is behaving oddly. He is cagey, at times friendly and direct, and at other times he will not meet my eye. I am confused by this behavior because our proposal is a very strong one. I can't understand why he isn't excited to do the deal and get down to business.

The plan is to set up a new company that will produce a first aid kit that can heal wounds using technology that until now could only be used in the top hospitals in the world. The goal would be to sell this cutting-edge product to the military, since it could make a critical difference in saving lives in remote field locations.

This is a product that would revolutionize health care and make an important difference in the world. The company would surely do very well. We are excited by the prospect. On our trip we see military personnel in the airport and on the street in San Juan.

■ ■ ■

I am proud to see them at work and I smile to myself and exchange glances with Ron. If only we could tell them of our plans to help protect them and keep them safe, even while they are working to keep us safe! It is a beautiful dream, and we both wish to fulfill it.

We finally speak of this when we settle in at our resort, just before his partner joins us. In the distance is the island of Vieques, famous for its military base. Ron explains to me the history of the American military in the region, and I am impressed as always with the depth of his knowledge. I know we make a very strong team.

Many young Puerto Ricans serve patriotically, he tells me, and there are bases he will show me in Florida as well, if I am interested. But I tell him that I do not need to see them all. I am convinced, and I see that his ties to the military are strong as is his vision. I respect that. I want to make this deal happen. We are both deeply committed. So it surprises me when, back in the hotel suite, after dinner, his partner seems so uninterested.

Our discussions have been going deeper and deeper

into the details of the deal. A few glasses of single-malt scotch have warmed the conversation, and I tell myself that the partner's distance is just a quirk of his personality, though I am not sure that I believe that. I am a little uneasy. Nevertheless, toward the end of the night, we forge an agreement and shake on it. It seems that it will work out after all.

It turns out I am right to feel uneasy: the next day the partner tells me that he wants to do the deal, and he wants my capital contribution, but only if we cut out Ron. My honor simply will not allow such a thing. He insists. I tell him business doesn't work like that. There is a code. We honor agreements; we treat our associates with respect.

■ ■ ■

Furthermore, I say, my voice swelling just a touch as I feel my anger rise at this injustice, I cannot do business with someone who has such little respect for a man who introduces him as a trusted partner. That man will not get my respect, and he will not get my money.

I tell Ron that we are leaving and that I will see him downstairs. It is too much to explain right away and I am frustrated and ashamed for my friend, who has behaved graciously, that his friend turned out not to be the gentleman he presumed he was. I am disappointed for him that his trust was so misused, and frankly I am a little bit perturbed that we have come all this way for things not to work out.

Only a little perturbed, however: in life, I find that one must always be on the lookout for the right deals. With success comes small disappointments, but when they bring me new insights, to new places, and to places as beautiful as this Caribbean island, overall I am grateful for what I have and of how far I have come. I tell Ron it is better to know now who his true friends are. We board the plane for Fort Lauderdale, where more business discussions await.

Back in Fort Lauderdale, Ron offers me his hospitality again, and this warms my heart. I feel it is better for me to check into a hotel, however, so as not to be too much of a burden on his family, who are so lovely to have taken me in as their guest. On LinkedIn, I find that my international reputation has continued to spread.

My connection to law enforcement and international espionage circles is growing. A top-level Interpol official has contacted me. I will call her Ivelisse. She is very striking looking, with dark eyes. I respond and she writes back right away. She is in Fort Lauderdale, too, she says.

Ivelisse comes to my hotel, which has a glamorous bar, with a waterfall in the background, elegantly touched off by a spotlight. It is a cool evening and she draws closer to me.

She reveals, confidentially, that she is in fact an investigator for Interpol. I am intrigued. She does criminal investigation in cross-border affairs, she tells me. I feel that she is attracted to my sharp mind.

She asks me questions about business, and I see that the connections I have made in New York and Zurich have given me quite a reputation. I remain vague. The mystery is compelling to her and it draws her in. I make her laugh. We have a connection, I can see. She comes to my room and we spend a romantic night together. The next morning she is gone.

I see later that she has defriended me on LinkedIn. This gives me pause. Did she come to investigate me? Perhaps to check me out on behalf of some government body or important people?

It is all very strange but I do not regret it for a moment. I know she enjoyed herself and I am confident that the impression I made was outstanding. I have nothing to hide. I am becoming a celebrity in international circles. People want to be close to me, to know me, to know the workings of my mind. They see my success and they value, honor, and admire that.

Ivelisse was a pleasure to know, if only for one night. She gives me insight into how my life is changing and a glimpse of what new horizons are opening to me. High level officials on the international scene are taking notice of me beyond Africa, beyond Europe, here in the Americas, in a new sphere of influence. My presence is felt and acknowledged. I feel good about this harbinger of new things to come.

Later that day, Ron comes to the hotel for lunch by the pool. He has another deal he wants to do, this time with a product for law enforcement. We will have to go to Virginia to meet with the founder of the company. I ask him if we are going to Virginia for national security reasons. Or is it because of the FBI, which has a large central facility in Quantico?

He smiles knowingly and there is a silence. He politely demurs. He cannot answer me, he says. Ron always knows more than he can say because of his connections, but there are times when sharing that information may put those connections at risk. I trust Ron.

I tell him I do not need to know. He smiles again, nods his head, and extends his hand to take mine in a gesture of our partnership. I think briefly of the business partner who tried to cut him out in San Juan. What were his motivations? What were his connections? Did he want to steer the business away from the interests of law and order and the United States to some other force or country? I feel good that I am still with Ron because I know his heart and I am confident he knows mine. On the plane to Virginia I pore over the documents for the product.

This next deal would also focus on a similar product, on the cutting edge of transplant technology. It uses a new material, replacing the silicone that is ordinarily used in certain operations. Former military scientists developed it. They are in talks with high-level law enforcement connections in Virginia and want to bring us on board for financing, marketing, and operations management. The scientists and their future CEO are very cool in their demeanor. I see a multibillion-dollar investment that will be placed for IPO, myself being CEO and the face of the company.

Ron is connected to them through his own law enforcement background, and unlike the business partner in San Juan, they strike me as straightforward, honorable people. They are relying on him to introduce him to good connections, and I see that the trust they have in him extends to me.

■ ■ ■

Unfortunately, after a few days of discussing the details, the deal breaks down. They need the capital right away in cash, and that is not possible. We part ways with scientists and the CEO, shaking hands and wishing one another well. Ron offers to accompany me back to New York and be my security detail but I decide that I prefer to go alone.

We shake hands and part ways amicably.

It has been an educational journey and he is a worthy business associate to know. I take a sleek black car to the airport to catch a first-class flight to JFK. I let my eyes gaze at the green palm trees and the setting sun as I turn my mind to what will come next, when I am back in wintry New York City. I have big plans to develop and much to think about. The deals that we pursued may not have come to fruition, but they are the kind of cutting-edge deals that situate me suitably in tech. They give me access to military and government circles. I am attracting important people into my life, and I am pleased. Even the next acquaintance I make demonstrates to me the truth of this conclusion.

On the plane, I settle in with a glass of champagne. They don't have the best champagne—it is an airplane after all—but it is proper French champagne and I am pleased with it. Seated beside me is a beautiful woman, petite, in her early 30s, with long dark hair, pale skin, and simple but very chic dark sunglasses. I smile at her and invite her join me in a drink. Her name is Brooke and she is a nuclear scientist living in New York.

She is very smart and listens attentively as I tell her about the different medical inventions I was looking to finance over the past two weeks. We laugh together. I can see that she likes me. Like me, she is well dressed, successful, educated, and she likes to talk and flirt. We become quite affectionate during the flight. Champagne always helps. We clearly have a connection. She gives me her home address before she goes off to her connecting flight.

While I was in Fort Lauderdale in early December, someone called Sesh contacted me via LinkedIn. He tells me how excited and he is by all the work I am doing and how proud he would be to have me as a business connection.

Sesh is British but he lives in India, in New Delhi, with his family. Because of this international focus, he calls himself a business diplomat. He tells me that he wants to work together. He does coaching. That's good, I say, okay. But really I have all of these business deals I am not pursuing. I am leaving money on the table because I have not been able to close the deals in Zurich, since I am unable to travel there.

That Zurich deal is worth $10 billion US. Even for someone as successful as I am, that is a huge deal, and I ache to complete it. I ask Sesh if he can help me do these deals. I tell him about Naomi and about the Swiss government, about all the curious and infuriating things that happened, and my resulting visa troubles there. We were just beginning these conversations when I landed back in New York.

Nick, a persistent real estate agent—I don't know how he got my number—had shown me a penthouse apartment at 88 Greenwich Street. It was an impressive place, and one I already knew, for it is the same building in which I had rented Sahel's apartment on Airbnb. We signed the lease earlier in the year, giving me a very good deal for six months, but the lease does not begin until January 1. Now it is Christmastime, and I decide to go to Atlantic City for a few days until the lease begins.

■ ■ ■

In Atlantic City it is cold by the sea, but the clubs and the casinos are full of glamorous people, many of them attractive women, dancing and flirting with me. Before I arrived, I made sure to book a high-end hotel with the most exclusive nightclub and restaurant on the premises. I wanted to have a good time, to treat myself to the finest things among beautiful people, and I wanted it all to be very convenient. After an aged Kobe steak and two Manhattans, I leave the restaurant feeling fantastic.

■ ■ ■

I take a short walk in the sea air and enter the club. In the center of the dance floor, by the bar, I see a group of five or six beautiful young women. The music is perfect, the bass just right, and the club is thrumming with excitement. Several of the women meet my eye and they draw me into their circle on the dance floor.

Before long we are laughing, coconspirators in a daring night out. They dance with me flirtatiously, closely. They buy me drinks. Sometimes I am not sure which one is dancing and which one is touching me. The dance floor feels electric with our collective pleasure.

Here at the seaside resort, deep in winter, we are riding waves of pleasure like surfers on a perfect beach day. They clearly all know each other and came to dance together. And they really like me, too. I am amazed at this magical turn of events. After so many boring nights I needed a bit of fun. It is as if I have walked into a party and I am the guest of honor! We order a few rounds and dance a few dances, new friends, happy, sexy, carefree.

Suddenly this all comes to a halt. Two very big guys, impeccably dressed, security guys or bouncers perhaps, come over and try to break up our group. Suddenly I feel all the enjoyment drain from the room. I get a sour taste in my mouth. I look over and see that they work for some older men sitting at a VIP table getting bottle service. They want the women to come sit with them. The two big security guys are a little rough with me as they block my way.

It isn't exactly violence but there is the threat of possible violence. I am irritated that they have soured the mood in the room. The women look sorry to go, and I can see why: those guys are clearly very rich, but they don't have my youthful good looks, fitness, or sense of style.

Frustrated, I head to the bar. A man there tells me that I should be careful, that some women are just here for money. I tell him I don't play that way, and I am not worried. I can have a good time and I don't pay for such things.

After a time, two of the women leave the VIP table and come sit with me. It is getting very late. We have a drink together and I learn their names. I am glad they have come back to me. Clearly this is where they would rather be! I buy a round of Manhattans. After a couple sips, the one closest to me asks if I would like them to come to my room. I smile. I knew this was what they wanted from me. I am a lucky man; women pursue me with some frequency.

When we get back to my room, the second woman looks at me in a new way, quite directly. She tells me I should pay them now, before anything happens. I tell them that I don't do that. I have no need to pay for things. Would they like to stay and have an amazing evening with me? I offer them caviar from the minibar, room service champagne. I won't pay, I tell them. That's not for me. They look at each other and shrug. Then they leave the room. What a strange experience! I marvel at their behavior. They were obviously having so much fun with me. But it is not my fault that they've made this decision. I peel back the covers on my king-sized bed and drift off into a deep sleep, dreaming of deals in Zurich and my new life among the global elite in New York.

CHAPTER TWELVE:

Hunted Across Continents

BACK IN NEW YORK, it is early January 2014. I am ill at ease in my new penthouse at 88 Greenwich Street. Something feels off. New York is dark and cold. The keycard to the gym in the building doesn't work. My Wi-Fi is very slow, suspiciously slow. It is slow in the way that only happens when someone has hacked your computer or the Wi-Fi itself. I know this from my years running IT companies, and I know it because of my experiences with intelligence agencies.

I have the background of a highly trained spy that I learned the hard way, looking over my shoulder from the age of eight for survival in the streets, and I am attuned to the world in such a way that I sense such things. I feel it is Naomi who is following me, infecting my computer.

I talk to Sesh about all these things. He is curious

about the Swiss government but I want him to focus on Naomi. I want to stay focused on what I want. It is a skill that has brought me great success in business and in life. I ask him if he will help me communicate with Naomi or the Swiss government.

Will he help me do these deals, including the $10 billion one in Zurich? He tells me he will. I hire him for $2,000. I am very unhappy in New York. Sesh advises me to go back to Johannesburg, then to Switzerland. I agree, and I break my lease.

Finally at home in Johannesburg, I am talking to Sesh every day. I tell him everything, the whole story. He says he thinks I should sue the Swiss government. I tell him I want to focus on Naomi instead, as that is the easy way out, marrying Naomi!

■ ■ ■

I ask him if he will go to her on my behalf, in Zurich. Will he approach her as my emissary, speak to her for me, tell her of my devotion and dreams for the two of us? Will he represent in the best way possible all that I can do for her and ask her to marry me? I want him to go and get Naomi's attention. I tell Sesh I don't know if it's a government or a person who is stalking me but I have to find out.

I give him $12,000 for airline tickets, accommodations, gifts, and other things. He asks me if he can use my credit card to buy some perfume for his wife. Then he goes to see Naomi. And I wait. I wait, knowing he is there in Zurich with the person who haunts me.

Finally, after many hours I hear from him. He says she has no answer for me. This is deeply perplexing. I do not understand. Sesh repeats, she has no answer. He tells me that Naomi says she wants to be friends. She tells Sesh that she knows who is stalking me, but that it is not her. This is very curious, and I don't know what to think of it. He says she showed him a picture, and it looks like her. What is she trying to say? I am confused by all of this. I worry again for her state of mind.

Naomi says that she wants me to go to therapy. We can be friends, she says, if I go to therapy. Now, I do a lot of what I call self-mediation in my life. Not self-medication, self-mediation. I mediate between the different forces, the drives and desires that pull me. I work with my thoughts just as I work with my body in the gym. I pay attention to my health in my body and in my mind. But if Naomi says I must go to a therapist so that we can be friends, I agree that I will try this for her, and I set about to find a therapist to see me. I call my friend Bernard, because he is wise and he knows a lot of smart people. He recommends a therapist. I tell Sesh to tell Naomi that I will go.

I truly didn't understand why I was being recommended to visit a therapist and started raising questions, as I felt that it was part of a game to drive me insane!

On the day of my appointment, I arrive eager, striving to be a good friend to Naomi. I tell the therapist about everything that has happened. I tell her about Naomi, about our night in the club, about our meeting when she ran away. I tell her I want to marry Naomi. She asks me how I feel about who I am. She tells me that I am strong in myself.

"I don't think I can help you," she says. "You are fine the way you are."

I report this back to Sesh, grinning ear to ear. I am fine the way I am! Of course I am.

Sesh tells me more of what Naomi is thinking. I begin to get suspicious of him. How did he come to find me in the first place? Why does he push me so much? Something is not quite right about this. With the mental clarity I have honed over decades in international business and law, I begin to see that it is likely that Naomi or the Swiss sent him to me to watch over me and control me, or perhaps even to test me.

Sesh says again that he thinks I should sue the Swiss government. I am beginning not to trust him, but I look into it. I call a lawyer and explain the situation. The lawyer says his retainer will be $50,000 just to hire him. I tell him that he cannot lose. They have lost me this $10 billion deal, and MBA to boot, which is worth even more, I am sure. He says he cannot help me without the $50,000. I think about the lawsuit and write a story to put on my website declaring that I will sue. Perhaps I can pressure them in this way, and we can avoid the hassle, the expense, and for them, the embarrassment of what they have done to me. The lawsuit would be worth $300 million, though what I have lost—the MBA, the $10 billion dollar deal, time with my beloved Naomi—is worth far more than that.

Finally, I look at my credit card bill. I am furious! Sesh has told me that he was going to buy some perfume for his wife for a gift, but he has bought enough bottles to start a perfume store! It is unbelievable. A total breach of trust. He should have bought maybe one or two bottles, not nearly this many! Is he giving gifts to an entire village? Or is he selling the perfume to make a profit? Either way, it is not what we agreed. He is taking advantage. I tell him I will not pay him any more money. Naomi was the one who paid him to come to me in the first place. Sesh and I fell out. He kept taking advantage. He should not have bought all of that perfume. I know he had direct contact with Naomi or the Swiss government and he was not on my side.

Meanwhile, in South Africa, I am contacted by *Leadership* magazine. It is the premier magazine on leadership in South Africa. They tell me that they want to interview me as a leader in business and politics and put my picture on the front cover. They are very proud of my work and want to feature my accomplishments. They only cover the top leaders in business and industry, and they want to feature my life story and insights as the centerpiece of their next issue.

I am very touched and humbled by this great honor. They tell me that they want to invite me to be a judge in their annual leadership convention, to be held at the Emperor Palace. They ask if I would like to address the conference as an honored speaker on a panel.

■ ■ ■

I tell them that I would be delighted to share my story and vision with them. I know that it can inspire many people from all walks of life to work hard and prosper in business. I think of myself as a boy, of how I benefited from the small bits of encouragement I received from adults who inspired me despite my father's absence.

■ ■ ■

I think of how meaningful and powerful a vision of a future with possibility can be to someone who might otherwise have nothing or might be tempted by a life of crime. Emotions swell in my heart as I think of this. I am grateful for my success.

Of course I will give all the time I can to help *Leadership* magazine showcase my story for young people just starting out.

We make an appointment for an interview and photo shoot at my Regus Virtual Office in Sandton City, South Africa. It is a beautifully appointed office suite with all the finest furnishings and equipment and wonderful light from wide, clear windows.

It is an office that showcases how far I have come in life, at the top of the business world with global investment and global reach, from poor beginnings in Ethiopia, and a small starter business here many years ago. The interviewer is smart and young.

She asks many intelligent questions and we get on quite well. I tell them my whole story, including the deals that fell through in Zurich and my struggles with the Swiss government. The photographer takes photos for the cover as well as to illustrate the story.

■ ■ ■

Once they are done, I send a letter to the Swiss embassy telling them about the story. The next day the *Leadership* magazine people call to tell me that they are very pleased with the story, but that they have contacted the embassy and cannot run it because of the lawsuit with the Swiss.

They withdraw the whole thing. I am very disappointed. I would have gladly accepted edits but they tell me it doesn't work that way. I feel as though people who might have learned so much and might have found so much inspiration will now be deprived of my story. It is truly a sad situation. I marvel at the power of the Swiss government, that the tentacles of their power can reach even a South African magazine and as far as the US.

The attaché from the Swiss embassy contacts me. His name is Marc. Marc has read my letter and he tells me that the Swiss are very sorry to hear about the trouble I had for cancellation of my study permit and the consequence.

He tells me that he will help me file a complaint so that this will never happen again. I am not sure whether this will resolve the matter but I am pleased that they are finally showing some concern. It is deeply vexing to me that I have lost out on the opportunities that *Leadership* magazine was offering due to the fallout of this misunderstanding with the Swiss government.

This matter could easily be rectified: instead they are blocking my business, I sigh to myself after I get off the phone with Marc. I hope to put this behind me soon. Switzerland was a wonderful country to me, and Zurich a place full of knowledge and possibility. I hope to rekindle such a mutually beneficial relationship with that city, with that country, and perhaps with one particular strikingly beautiful, intelligent citizen: Naomi.

■ ■ ■

I now feel ready to return to the United States. I feel stymied and blocked in all the good I want to do right now, and a change of scene seems like the right thing. Like a shark, I must keep moving, keep searching. Sesh was not a good connection, though he was well spoken and seemed fantastic at first. Whether he was paid by Naomi or the Swiss government to play me and control me or he simply was not an especially honorable man, he took up my energy and ultimately did not help solve my problems.

Leadership magazine had a wonderful plan to use my story to inspire others, and yet that too was blocked by my problems with the Swiss government. These problems should be resolvable by reasonable people.

I am making my best efforts in good faith and yet there is something stopping me. It is springtime in Washington, DC, and I want to spend some time there and have some meetings with people.

I would like to see how I can form alliances and partnerships to work with government, in order to grow my business and contribute to international trade in the global business community.

I book my ticket for the trip to DC. On board the plane, champagne in hand, my heart soars with it into the heavens toward my next adventure.

CHAPTER THIRTEEN:

Dirty Play and Overcoming the Distractions

WHILE DOING my preliminary research in Washington, D.C., I receive a LinkedIn message from a very well-connected, well-to-do businesswoman named Maggie. Among other things she runs an art gallery and a horse farm in Connecticut.

She is sharp, savvy, and would like very much to network with me and do business. She is looking for investors for a company related to her art gallery. She would like to present a deal to me, with an initial investment of $50,000.

There is a stylish arts component to this company as well as an educational side, and it also had a project for disadvantaged children. I find this all very appealing, because I believe in the arts, and I believe in giving back. I also think that a company can do these things and still make a profit.

I am attracted to the idea of investing in a company that will connect me to the young, smart set at the center of cultural life in New York, where Maggie is based. These are people I want to connect with, educated people like me who love the arts and who care about others. I am very intrigued and want to learn more.

Maggie tells me that I should leave DC and come to New York. She tells me that I should rent a place for her, me, and her sister to share. I ask, "Who is your sister?" She sends me a photo. It looks just like Naomi: blond, pale skin, blue eyes, chiseled features.

■ ■ ■

Ah, I say to myself. This is interesting. Is it Naomi? It looks an awful lot like her. Perhaps this is why Maggie is contacting me. Maybe it is an arranged marriage by the Swiss government.

I spend some time looking at the picture and think about some unexplained messages I have received lately from unknown numbers. Perhaps this is the heart of the real deal Maggie wants to execute. I rent an apartment on Airbnb for all of us to share in Brooklyn as she requested, and I book a first class ticket on a luxury shuttle flight to New York.

When I arrive at the apartment, this girl opens the

door. Supposedly she is Maggie's sister, but her face is far too familiar. I am stunned into silence, and so, I think, is she. Is it Naomi? Is that why she is acting this way, too, like she, too, has waited many months for us to be reunited and at last we are? The air in the room seemed heavy with meaning.

It was awkward, the silence. We don't know whether to hug or kiss or shake hands. I started talking about all the things I did for her—for Naomi—while I was in South Africa. The house I rented for her and decorated at great expense. I spent so much of my hard-earned money hoping that it would bring to an end the plight of my life, the stress I caused my family, and the blocking of my effort to make this world a better place for all to live fairly and equally.

The emissaries I sent with gifts of jewelry, watches, and a promise of a ring. I'm observing how she behaves through all of this. I take in her emotional response with the keenly attuned senses of a ninja, something I picked up in intelligence circles I learned from the street and from expert martial artists I knew in the prison in Tanzania.

■ ■ ■

Whether in situations of international espionage or while serving time in a tough prison, the skills of the mind are as important as those of the body. One keeps silent and observes all the signs of others, like the big cats of the jungle where my grandmother had her home when I was a boy. I have learned from all these experiences how to attune my senses and my mind, and so I watched, I listened, and I waited. I took it all in.

She looks a lot like Naomi. Her face, her hair, her eyes—they are all the same or very nearly so. But she has a different name now, a Russian name, Evgenia. Her manner is also noticeably different.

Wondering why I have been set up with a replica of Naomi. Placing myself at risk with someone who is able to poison or kill me in whatever way. I started asking myself so many questions and thinking about possible solutions of how to end things and indeed, fighting with her was not a solution and I was convinced to find who she was working with and that would happen only without frightening and having to keep sleeping with her.

I tell her more and more and more of all my hopes for us, of all the times I reached out, of all the times I knew she was there, reaching out to me, and she crumbles a bit, like a fragile bird, with emotion, and while telling her all this story I see a confusion in her face. I could see that I had confused her with someone she is not.

Tears well up in her face. I take her in my arms, gently, and feel the tears well up in mind. She makes her body small as I hold her. We are both crying. We stay that way for five minutes? Ten minutes? Several days?

■ ■ ■

It is hard to tell when she can be broken so she can tell me all, but the clock's hands only move two inches. I hear her breathing like a small child, frightened by the power of everything we have between us.

After some time, she says very quietly in her Russian accent, her voice like a whisper, "I need to go outside and get some air."

I go into my bedroom and meditate for 30 minutes, hoping to hear what I wanted to hear . . . that she has mulled it over and doesn't know even how that news could help me!

When she comes back, she seems more even-tempered, more resolved. After my meditation and shower, my mind is once again well attuned and my body is clean and fresh after the journey. I am rested, eager to pick things up where I left off in Zurich.

She proposes a walk and a glass of wine. We go out together, hand in hand, like we have never been apart.

"Well," I say when we are seated at a charming Italian café. I look into those eyes that have seen so many men and say it again, "Well."

Her name is Evgenia, she says, but if I want I can call her Naomi. I know in my bones. Or maybe she is telling me that she has been paid and set up to distract me from my past I wish to pursue.

I am having fun, and she is a beautiful companion, laughing and openhearted, and she listens to me with all her attention. We go to one club and then the next. We dance, close together, flirtatiously. We make each other laugh.

■ ■ ■

When we return to the apartment, Maggie has locked herself in one of the bedrooms. There is only one other bedroom and the couch. Evgenia elects to stay with me, in the bedroom. I think some days when she goes out they change places, and she can say, "Oh, I went shopping," or, "Oh, I went to the salon," to explain why she looks a little different and trying to convince me that she is Naomi as if they found my weak point.

Maggie doesn't offer any explanation. She doesn't talk about any deal or any art business. She doesn't talk to me at all, really. She just disappears.

Maggie, in fact, is gone. She has disappeared without a word. A new person arrives in the apartment, another beautiful young woman. Her name is Anna, she says, and she is from Austria, but I know, my mind tells me, that she is Swiss intelligence. She has the same model phone I have seen used by European intelligence officers and also the same black Tumi holdall.

Tumi is a common brand but this bag is rare. I saw it when I was working with law enforcement at the highest level. The Interpol woman had it, too. I can see I am still famous in these circles. They come and go around me but I can tell they are observing me, too.

After two weeks in Brooklyn, we move to the Standard. It is the perfect time of year to stay there, in late spring, before the tourists arrive. The glamorous rooftop bars and the club with the Jacuzzi pool are perfect for warm, sexy nights of cocktails and fashionable people. The music is divine. The scene is ever shifting, always with new people, gorgeous people moving through, drinking, dancing, laughing.

■ ■ ■

Many of them must be there for Fashion Week, I am sure. They are the international fashion set. I have a stunning woman on my arm and I feel on top of the world at times. I still wonder if she is Naomi. When I am with her and I feel that she is Naomi, the woman of my dreams, then we are connected. Everything is real and as it should be. But at those moments when I am not so sure, our connection fades. My love is for Naomi.

Strange things happen when I am with this woman, things I cannot account for properly. Wherever we go, whatever hotel, we get an upgrade that we didn't deserve. She is always smiling and laughing. Why? Who is she laughing with? The clerks at the hotels' front desks seem to be laughing, too. What is happening here? I am paying $700 a night for the Palace. That is an incredible deal. I have never heard of such a deal. Even though I booked on Hotels.com, there is no way you can get a room at the Palace for that. These people behind this, they must have a lot of resources.

When I'm with Evgenia, I get these anonymous messages, but I also get messages from European societies, inviting me to join. I get an email from a secret society in Lichtenstein, telling me that I have the kind of international profile of success that they look for in new members.

Lichtenstein is a very small, old country, with an elegant high society profile. If I am being asked to join a secret society for the elite, this will be a very small club, indeed, possibly including members of the royal family.

It is not the first time I am asked to keep company with royalty. I consider it an honor and a reflection of all the work I have done that people from noble families recognize the fine substance I have inside me. It is humbling indeed to get recognition for one's accomplishments.

Lichtenstein, I might add, shares its entire western border with Switzerland. Spending time in Lichtenstein, I would not be far from the eyes of Swiss intelligence, which have even sent someone to share an Airbnb with me.

Evgenia clearly plays some role here. She giggles when I tell her about it and pretends to be surprised, but I know she is faking.

"Who are you?" I implore her to tell me.

"I am Evgenia form Russia!" she declares. "I have a background in the financial industry."

This last part I am not sure about. I think she wants us to have more in common, so she says this. But she swears that in Russia she worked in finance and that in the US she is only waiting to pass her exams to do something similar here.

One night she tells me she wants to get married. I say, I am not going to marry you! I do not even know who you are! You say you are Evgenia but then why do you know so much about Naomi? Why do you look so much like her, have German-speaking friends, and sometimes sound like your accent might come from Switzerland as well? Why do you act so strangely around me? I am getting more and more suspicious, and a little weary from it all.

After a certain point in time, I get tired of the games. I see through her fake smiles. I wonder whom she is talking to on her phone. Who is she texting? We are in the Palace again, after staying in about ten different hotels, each with their mysterious too-friendly laughing front desk agents, each with their unbelievable discounts.

"Who are you?" I shout at her one day in frustration. I have so many questions. I snatch at her passport and take a picture of it. I am fed up. I need to know.

She gets upset with me for taking the picture. She is yelling, crying. Her face is red and she is a mess. I tell her I am sending it to Ron, who was formerly with NYPD and still has many connections in law enforcement. She gets more pissed off. She is crying even more.

"Who do you think you ARE?" she shrieks at me. "A god?"

I see that she recognizes my power and I am sad for her that she is so upset, but I need to know.

When Ron gets back to me, things have calmed down a bit in our hotel room. We are drinking wine from room service, not quite friends again, but sitting quietly and eyeing ear other warily. We are both exhausted from the fighting and the games. Ron reports to me that immigration does not know that she is in the country. I decide to scare her a little more so that she will not want to be with me, and I tell her what Ron has said. It works. She packs her things up in plastic grocery bags and leaves the hotel. I give her some money to tide her over for a while, a few thousand dollars.

When Evgenia asked me that, if I thought I were a god, she came close to seeing the angels that watch over me. This is something many others have told me, and clearly it is true. I have been through so many things in my life, so many things, and yet I survive. I should be dead or in jail or a billionaire by now.

I truly have angels watching me from above, protecting me from dangerous forces. I am grateful for this every day. I know it is a special gift I have been given, to be so blessed. That is why I dedicate my life to using my gifts to bring good things into the world, to fight for what is right, and to protect those who need protection.

■ ■ ■

After that, Evgenia just disappeared. I am left wondering what is going on. We spent six weeks together in New York that summer, and now—poof—she is not there any longer.

Ron congratulates me on making a break with Evgenia. It was time, he said. He tells me, "You have done a lot for Naomi."

He tells me that he will go to Zurich now, on my behalf, another emissary and perhaps the most trusted one I can send. He will meet with Naomi and find out the truth about what has been going on.

He will try to convince her to come back to New York with him, or to have me visit her, perhaps meeting her in Milan, and if she agrees, I will buy her a ticket. I like this plan and I feel good about it. Several days pass and finally Ron calls me. He apologizes with his whole heart. He cannot go to Zurich. His passport is expired and his family needs him there at the moment. He suggests I try to move on with my life and put Naomi behind me. It is clean advice from the heart of a true friend. I want to take it, but it seems that the mystery still has a hold on me and I wonder why I am being stalked and set up with people who intend to distract me from progressing in my life.

Evgenia and I lose touch for a while, until she sends me a message one day and says that she is homeless. I wonder where her money comes from and who is paying her bills until now. The picture she senses shows her feet in terribly worn out shoes. Her feet are bleeding.

It moves me to tears, especially because of the charity I created to focus on providing shoes to poor children in Africa. No one should suffer for want of shoes. I remember my family struggling when I was young and this always breaks my heart. I send her money, one or two thousand dollars.

At some point down the road, she tells me that she lives in Zurich, Switzerland.

I think this is very interesting, because this is where

Naomi lives. I start wondering again. We have a Skype conversation. She tells me almost nothing. We have our differences and part ways again.

I decide that it is time to leave New York to go pursue some deals, and maybe some fun in Las Vegas. She said that she had no money, but she follows me to Las Vegas. I ask her, "Why have you come here? What do you want?"

She is staying at the most expensive places, and before she told me that she had no money.

"Who is paying for this?" I ask her. I am tired of being so confused.

She is staying in the highest-end hotels like the Cosmopolitan. Only the wealthiest people can afford that hotel. Someone is paying for her, for her to stay in such an expensive place. I want to know who this is. Is there another man? Are there many other men? Is she set up by the Swiss government?

I decide to drive to via Los Angeles to San Francisco by renting a car, a Suburban, to look into some tech companies and properties. Evgenia is calling me, messaging me and offering to meet me in Egypt, in the resort city Leth for a holiday. Why, I wonder? Does she think I am fooled by this? Then she says that afterwards we will fly to Milan and rent a car, to drive together to Zurich. To Zurich? Does everything lead back to Switzerland? Why is she now trying to lure me to return to Switzerland, when

the Swiss have been blocking all my deals and advance-
ment? I don't understand.

PART IV

A Global Business Mogul Lands in the Hollywood Spotlight

CHAPTER FOURTEEN:

*Good Friends Make the California Sunshine
That Much Warmer*

EVEN THOUGH MY SUCCESS has been first and foremost in the business world, on both local and global scales, and in making deals in that go well beyond business in areas like politics and diplomacy, I always say I would be nowhere in my life without the people who care for me and the angels watching over me.

Business is, like everything else, working with people. If you cannot work with people, if people do not respect you, you will be not get very far at all. The world can be a cold, demanding place, fraught with difficulty, and we need one another to band together and lift ourselves up.

Through all of the struggles I have faced, all of the adverse and almost impossible conditions, I have been blessed at every turn to make friends and allies even at the most unexpected moments and in unlikely places. These allies fight at my side and protect me. They shine warmly on me and offer their friendship and comradery. I have received the gift of their friendship, at times weary from my own struggles, and am astonished every time that this gift is there for me. I want only to repay it and to continue to be worthy of it.

There is no time when it is more valuable to have reliable, faithful friends and allies than when you move to a new part of the world, to a new city, and begin the difficult work of finding the lay of the land and making your way.

Every place is different. The people have different customs. There are new things to learn about how to succeed in that place, and you have to learn them even while you are fighting to survive. To do all of this alone is very difficult. Therefore, when the angels watching over me send me friends to fight alongside me and build me up, I know once again that I am blessed. I recognize this whenever I see it, the generosity of a new friend, and it touches my heart deeply. It is for this reason that I am always giving back, to inspire others and to help people who are suffering. I am so very blessed with true friends and allies that it moves me to share the blessings.

No one exemplifies this more in this moment in my story than my good friend Dick Michaels, who was there to guide me in Hollywood when I first started making my way there. It was time for me to move on from New York. The time I spent with Evgenia, who was not Naomi, sapped my energy. She gave me her love, it is true, and she wanted to be with me, but she was not who she seemed. It took a lot of energy from me to go through that, and I needed to recharge. She had a lot of connections in New York. And something was telling me that it was time to switch things up, as people say, to try a new field. To make my way in the movies.

As a very creative person, a successful, intuitive, creative person, I crave the excitement of change. I want to find new worlds, to learn new things. Wherever I go, people are amazed by the things I have done. They are amazed by my story, which has spanned so many languages and so many worlds. Women from all over the world, from every nation, have shown interest in me. I need to keep moving sometimes. My creativity gets blocked if I stay in one place for too long. I need the fresh energy that comes from seeing new vistas and forging new plans, bringing new things into the world that make people think. I need to express myself in new ways.

That is my freedom, and my gift, but also sometimes a burden that I struggle with. So I come back to the gratitude I have for the angels in my life, who believe in me and help carry me, and I come back, in my story, to my friend, Dick Michaels.

Dick Michaels is a truly special guy. Dick has been in Hollywood for many years. He is actually more than 80 years old, but you wouldn't think this if you saw his energy level and how sharp his mind is. He is a smart guy and he knows how Hollywood works. He is known most of all for his work in television, going back to its golden age. He has been a director and writer on many famous projects from the 1950s through the 1990s, when he retired but began to work behind the scenes. He was featured in the *E! True Hollywood Story* documentary on the famous television show *Bewitched,* on which he was a director for many years.

It is a well-known fact of Hollywood history that he had a romance with the glamorous star of that show, Elizabeth Montgomery. He has nearly 50 years of credits in Hollywood. You might say that Dick is a bit unstoppable, too! In his retirement, he has continued to network in the television and movie industries, taking meetings, listening to pitches, funding projects, doing deals, and encouraging others.

He is still invited to the best premieres and parties. He knows a lot of people, and he knows how to do business in this industry. I have nothing but respect for that. He keeps his hand in the game, just enough, while still relaxing and enjoying the benefits of his success. He is an elder statesman of Hollywood, eminently accomplished, seasoned, and kind enough to share his wisdom about the field to those looking to try their hand. It must have been one of my best, wisest angels who sent Dick Michaels to me.

I'm getting ahead of myself here, but I can't help but think first of the people who helped me to get started in Hollywood.

I should begin back at the beginning, when I first got to Los Angeles. I came out to California partly because I knew that there were many successful young people that a global business player like me should get to know. I also came to visit Brooke, the nuclear scientist I met on the first-class flight from Fort Lauderdale back when I was looking at deals with Ron. In Los Angeles, I took meetings with many important business people. There was a $1 billion real estate deal I was looking at through the agent that got me my first place there. He told me that as soon as he saw me, he knew I might be the right person for this deal.

I rented an apartment in downtown LA on Wilshire Boulevard, not far from the Standard, a very stylish area. The address was 1100 Wilshire. Terrence Howard, the actor from the hit TV show *Empire*, was my neighbor. It was a very up-and-coming area, and the vibe was very young, chic, and successful. It felt like a good place to start out. I rented a Porsche Cayenne and began to acclimate myself to the neighborhood.

Soon after I moved in, I made a connection with

Jennifer, the property manager. She was a kind of gate-keeper to life in Los Angeles for me. She was very well connected. We became close and she came over to my apartment every day. Like a lot of women in Los Angeles, for Jennifer, taking care of her appearance meant that sometimes she would have a little work done. She looked good, though. She had a very high-end lifestyle and she liked me.

The problem was that she was married. I liked Jennifer well enough to spend time with her, but I told her, I don't have sex with married women. It just goes against what I believe in. She and her husband have a child together. She doesn't like him, though, and she is interested in me, I can tell. She knows I am going to be a billionaire.

Her husband, it turns out, is very famous himself. He is very well-connected in politics, a high-end Washington lobbyist. Jennifer is also the gatekeeper of a $1 billion project and she wants me in on the deal. I am trying to be diplomatic and keep our relationship, our friendship, but I tell her that she has to understand that I won't be with a married woman, even if her husband is in Washington, DC, for most of the year. It just goes against my values.

She keeps telling me about the project but I can tell she wants more than this. Her last boyfriend was an NBA player, very fit, successful, good looking, and black. Jennifer was herself an LA Laker girl, a cheerleader for the

NBA team.

I was interested in the deal she was brokering but I also knew that her husband was very powerful. I told her about what happened in Switzerland and she became angry with me. She did not want to hear about Naomi or about the Swiss government. She tried to bring me into her family's oil businesses but I was very wary of her interest in me, given that she was married and her husband was so powerful.

After a while in Los Angeles, I went back to South Africa to celebrate my daughter's birthday. My daughter, Elinor, is the light of my life. She is absolutely brilliant in school, winning awards for the top student. Her face, to me, shines brighter than any diamond. It doesn't matter where I am. I wouldn't miss her birthday for the world. While I was in South Africa, I kept getting messages that said, *Los Angeles needs you. You will be a billionaire!* I knew in my heart that I belonged there now, so I returned to make a go of it.

His Excellency Kassa Tekelbeerihan Gebrehiwot, Speaker of the House of the Federation of the Federal Democratic Republic of Ethiopia, led a delegation to Ottawa and Toronto at the invitation of Noël Kinsella, Speaker of the Senate, and his visit to South Africa was similar in purpose, with an invitation from the South African government. I met him when he visited South

Africa for two days.

Kassa asked a lot of questions. He was very detailed in his inquiries. I told him everything I knew, and everything I suspected. They were angry about what was happening in Switzerland. Somehow they knew about all of it. This was why it was arranged for us to meet.

After many hours of conversation, I could see that they understood me and admired my work. I was very honored by this, because I want what is best for Ethiopia, and I was moved that they were looking out for me. They were thinking of me, but we were all thinking of the future of our country. Kassa and the secretary liked my mind-set.

They told me that they had never met anyone of my caliber before who was so young and so successful on such a large scale. They were impressed with my worldliness and knowledge, that I had come from such a small place and had had such huge success in South Africa and then in Europe.

They wanted to support me. Kassa said, "You are an upcoming future leader for our nation, Tariku. We need someone like you to take over our developing economy." They had a $4 billion project to take over the power stations and sell the power. "The future belongs to you," they told me. "We take all of these matters you have discussed with us very seriously."

Soon after that the secretary had a meeting with the

Swiss ambassador in Ethiopia. He called me from the meeting and passed the phone to her. I told the Swiss ambassador to Ethiopia what happened to me in Switzerland. She was very sincere and apologized to me. She said, "I'm sorry. This should not have happened." She told me to send her an email detailing the incident. She wrote back to me after that and said she was sending it to Bern.

After that she sent me a link to use to file a formal complaint, to communicate directly with Bern. I knew that as polite as she was, this meant that she was not going to help me. That was all I got from her. She should have supported my initiative because I was going to bring important, big deals with me, which would be big business for Switzerland and would connect the Swiss to African business. She should have recognized how important this could be for her country and her economy. Instead she said she would refer the matter to her government in Bern and that she could do no more.

Following this, it was clear that my profile on the international political stage as a global businessperson had been raised once again. Soon after, I was invited by Israeli homeland security to attend an exclusive conference showcasing Israeli capability in military defense and unmanned robotic technology. Special arrangements were made for me to meet with major corporate decision makers and high-level government officials. Once again, just like with

Ron, my connections were drawing me into the elite nexus of global business, politics, and high-level military technology. Only the highest-caliber people are admitted into this world, and I had now been invited more than once to participate. I felt proud and excited. It was clear that many high-level people strongly believed that I had the mind-set and capability to contribute to this exclusive world.

At the last minute, after I had made my travel arrangements for the conference, I received an email advising me that the conference had been postponed. My destiny, it seemed, drew me back once again then to Los Angeles.

■ ■ ■

When I returned to Los Angeles, this time I rented a place in West Hollywood. I met a young princess from a royal Saudi family, Sarah. This was a very interesting coincidence because at the time I had some dealings with Saudis in Dubai, partly as a result of my old ForEx business. I was also very interested in investing in oil and other natural resources, because oil powers the world.

My interest in Sarah, though, was much more pleasure than business, if you see my meaning—though of course beautiful women become many times more beautiful to me when they are smart and interested in success, like I am. Like me, Sarah was studying for her MBA. She was

Saudi by nationality but had grown up in Qatar and now lived in Los Angeles.

As a princess, she was of royal blood. Sarah didn't behave in any stereotypical way that you might think of when you think of Saudi people. She was very wealthy, of course, and was driving a big Porsche Cayenne. She also likes to take sexy selfies and post them to her Instagram and Facebook, showing off her tattoos. This is not traditional behavior for a Saudi princess! This is one of the things I love about Los Angeles; the people will surprise you, and most of the time in good, exciting ways.

Sarah and I met at a very glamorous party at the Hotel Bellagio, one of the places where I like to spend a lot of time in when I'm in LA, because the people are as high caliber and as beautiful as the setting. It comes as no surprise to me that I met someone like Sarah there. The morning after I met Sarah at that party, she introduces me to her father, the sheik. He invites me to come to Dubai to talk business sometime. The sheik recognizes that I am a businessman of the world, like him, and that I operate in many countries and industries. We share a moment of mutual respect and recognition.

Sarah has access to the private club at the Chateau Marmont, which is one of the top places to stay in Los Angeles, located on Sunset Boulevard, in a very glamorous area. One night when we go there, I find once again that my jacket has been stolen. This is a very curious thing, because it has happened to me a lot.

I wonder what it is that people think they will learn about me if they steal my jacket. Someone, I don't know who, maybe military intelligence or the Swiss government, is stealing my jackets. I wonder if they have put some-thing in there to track me. Someone has a collection of my jackets. Sometimes I worry that it is someone who wants to use some magic on me, so they take something that has been close to my body. I am very unsettled by it when it happens yet again.

I tell Sarah all of this. I tell her about Naomi, about Zurich, about the people following me in New York. At first I can tell she thinks it isn't real but after a while, after I explain about Birtukan and my involvement in politics and human rights, she gets nervous. We have an-other drink and make each other laugh.

Then, when we go out to my car, when we open the car, there is another woman's handbag in it! It is a very expensive leather handbag, Balenciaga, if I recall correctly. But it does not belong to Sarah, and it certainly does not belong to me. We look at the bag, then we lock the door and step away. Sarah starts breathing very fast, hyper-ventilating. She tells me that she sometimes thinks some-one is following her, too. I wonder if she is going to be all right. She looks very worried.

I tell the valet that this is not my bag and it is not my friend's bag. I try to get him to take it but he won't, so we go home. But then my phone buzzes, later that night, and it is a WhatsApp message from an unknown number in South Africa. *You have the wrong bag*, the message says.

In the morning, Sarah was gone. This incident made her very nervous, I think, or perhaps someone was threatening her because she was with me. I can almost understand why they might want my jackets, because I know a lot about the technology that is available. I do not understand the meaning of the bag.

Because of Sarah's family connections to the business world and her studies as an MBA student in Los Angeles, she knew about a lot of important networking opportunities. She invited me to attend the California Business Summit with her. It was interesting to attend a conference like this in Los Angeles, because people have a very different style of doing business in California. It is far less formal than New York or Johannesburg or Zurich, but that doesn't mean that it isn't serious.

In California, people like to wear simple, casual clothes. Sometimes those clothes are very expensive, even if it is just a pair of jeans and a hoodie. They may be the most expensive jeans you can buy. In New York or Zurich or Johannesburg, that person would be wearing a suit to signify their high status. But even in a hoodie, you can shake hands on a multimillion-dollar deal. I prefer myself to wear classic clothes, a beautiful suit jacket, a hand-tailored shirt. (This is perhaps why so many of my jackets are stolen!) I favor a classic look, but a fashionable one. I enjoy the latest styles, and this is also something you find in California.

At the California Business Summit, I wore a tailored suit made by a local fashion house. I could tell people were impressed by me and I exchanged business cards with a lot of people and sat in on a few seminars for investors in real estate.

At the summit, just after one of the seminars ended, Sarah introduced me to her boss, Percy, over a drink at the hotel bar. Percy is a dangerous guy, some say a cleaner, if you know what that means. He exudes an air of violence. Put just one foot over the line, his body language and glowering face seem to say, and that will be the end of it. He would snap you in two over nothing and you can sense it. He wants you to sense it. He uses this to his advantage.

I don't like violence. I am a peaceful warrior, as others have told me. I always keep very fit, through proper physical training and eating the healthiest foods, but I don't have any need to show off my strength like Percy does. I don't need everyone to be afraid of me all the time. I don't have to show my power in such a vulgar way. I'm not really impressed when someone acts like this, and I don't particularly want to be very close to someone who presents himself the way Percy did that day.

I don't want any violence or ugliness clouding my vision, taking away from my purpose, or worst of all, hurting anyone. Percy works for the government. This we know. Or maybe it is more than one government that hires him when they need him. Or maybe he works mostly for himself. It is hard to say and I am not that motivated to find out. I want to keep ugliness out of my life, if I can. Something about him says BAD NEWS. But I am getting ahead of myself.

That day, at the summit, while we were talking, Percy accused me of being a spy. He said that I was a rat and that I should leave the United States! This was a very shocking thing to say and obviously an unacceptable way to behave in a cordial business atmosphere. I can conjure no earthly reason that he would say such a thing except to intimidate me.

I think perhaps he has heard of me in international circles and he is threatened by my success. Or perhaps he is nervous that I will find about something he is doing and speak to my connections in law enforcement or military intelligence about his activities. Perhaps he can sense how finely attuned my mind is through years of training. I do not know why he says I am a rat and should leave the country. I do know, however, that he is Italian and German, and I start to think that maybe on the German side he is close to the Swiss.

He yells at me and makes these shocking accusations. I am sick of this treatment. It happened too much in New York, and here I am in Los Angeles, and again someone is stealing my jackets and I am being told that I am up to no good and should go home. I decide to stand up to Percy and show him that I will not be intimidated. I shout back at him and bang my fist on the table.

"I will leave when I want to leave, and not a minute before!" I bark at him. My nature is to be peaceful and kind but I can be aggressive if it is warranted by the situation, I assure you. "Who do you think you are?" I yell at him.

Everyone at the table looks very nervous. An Australian business associate of mine, Serff, looks very nervous. He is clearly concerned for my safety. Everyone is very surprised. No one stands up to Percy. He gets away with acting like this all the time, I can tell. Everyone accepts his aggressive behavior. I will not tolerate that, I decide. I won't be disrespected like that.

I have come too far in life and even at my young age, I have lived through more than even Percy will ever see. The shouting makes everyone at the table tense. The waiter comes to intervene, and we all go our separate ways.

I go to the gym, which is what I like to do when things are difficult. I have a workout, a sauna, and a massage. I have worked hard to get where I am in life. I don't deserve this aggravation.

During my massage, as my muscles relax, I decide that I will approach Percy with an olive branch. We do not need to be fighting with one another. It is stupid to fight when you have mutual associates and interests. It is always better to make alliances, even if you cannot be close to everyone. I like to leave things on positive terms with people. I don't need any messes in my life. This philosophy has served me well in business and in international circles as well.

When I got home, I texted Percy. I imagine he was very surprised to hear from me. I don't think a lot of people stand up to Percy and I don't think many have the good manners to suggest reconciliation, either. This is just something I know from life experience. Most people are not like this. They either lack the manners or they lack the necessary self-assurance to carry themselves this way. I suggest to Percy that we meet up and have a cordial conversation. I tell him that I would like to be on polite, friendly terms with him and not to be at war. He texts back and agrees. We know too many people in common to be adversaries. It would not be healthy for anyone. We decide that we will meet at an elegant Japanese restaurant and share a meal, as a gesture of peace.

This is a strategic move on my part, a key move that I

learned through all my years in business. I will share this secret with you. It is a powerful one, so pay attention. If I am connected to Sarah, who is in business, I should be on good terms with all of her associates and her father's associates as well.

You should spread positivity throughout your network so that conversation, ideas, alliances, partnerships, deals, and the resulting successes can flow. If you make an enemy, you will have a block in that flow. You will block off one of the avenues that can bring you success. If I had made an enemy of Percy, I would have had a big, ugly road-block in one of my connections that flows through Sarah. Any success that could come my way from there would be stopped up.

That block can spread like a pile of garbage and bring down anyone it touches. It can sour the connections around it. In that way, it can kill deals. Now, sometimes a person can only be an enemy. Some people are like that. In that case you have no choice. I decided, based on my intuition and experience, that Percy had terrible manners and was aggressive and petulant like a little boy in a tough-guy costume, but he did not have to be my enemy.

Accordingly, we go out to dinner the next night. At dinner I tell him about my situation with the Swiss government. He listens. I don't know if it is the story that has changed his attitude or something else, but he asks me many detailed questions. Maybe someone has talked to him and now he knows more about who I am. Whatever change has taken place, he is showing me a new level of respect, one, frankly, that he ought to have shown me out of common courtesy at the California Business Summit.

You should always meet everyone with respect. But I have forgiven him his rudeness. He tells me that he will use his connections to try to help me with my difficulties.

He will call people he knows who have themselves have connections to high-level Swiss officials and he shows me pictures he had with the Russian president, Vladimir Putin. He calls the mayor of Los Angeles right in front of me, and always boasts about the number of billionaires he knows in Las Vegas and elsewhere to show me the connections he has. I truly didn't understand why he was carrying five phones, each of them loaded with so many young women's nude pics, which he shows me now and then, asking if I like one of them.

Percy was now my ally, and told me he would use his connections. He said he would rent a private plane for us to fly to Bern together to meet with Swiss officials through his connections. I happily agreed. I waited and waited but it never happened.

After that he was always keeping tabs on me. He always wanted to know where I was. Because of his work with the government, he is able to do that. I am not afraid of Percy but we are not going to be the best of friends, either. Still, this allows the positive energy to flow in my network and does not block possibility or success. I am cordial with Percy but still cautious. I observe people carefully. This, too, is important for success.

One night when I was staying at Le Méridien in Santa Monica, I went out to party. I was driving a beautiful Cabriolet convertible. I went to a very high-end, up-market club with dancing. A lady was staring at me. She was there with two other friends for a girls' night out. I could tell from her body language that she was inviting me to come across the room to meet her.

The three women were very friendly to me. They were dressed beautifully but simply, not too over the top but appropriate to a California beach community. They had a simple elegance about them. They bought me shots, really delicious shots, and we danced together, everyone, the four of us, all of us having a good time. I could tell that the woman who had looked at me was well known in the area because of the way that people greeted her.

At some point we stopped dancing and the two of us separated from the group to talk. She tells me her name is Trista and we talk about our lives a bit. I tell her that I am from South Africa and she is very admiring of this. Trista tells me that she has always wanted to go to South Africa because she has heard how beautiful it is there, but she has never been. She tells me that she works with children, helping them. I tell her that I also help children through my foundation. I feel close to her because we both care about this, and we have shared something important in our hearts with one another.

Trista suggests that we go for a walk on the beach, and we do, holding hands, and telling each other things. She's like a pure angel, very clean. I can see that she is becoming emotional. She is starting to cry. She tells me that she never does this. I realize that she is a public figure and holds herself to very high standards, and here she is alone on a beach with someone she has just met, and we are becoming intimate. I felt very close to her then because I understood that like me she has very high standards for herself. I can tell that we recognize each other.

We had sex on the beach and then we went back to my room at Le Méridien. She is an amazing person, so full of care for others. She shows me pictures of her school's children where she teaches, and she is kind of public figure, worried so much about being seen with unknown man in the community. We understood one another and made a real connection. In the morning she has to leave early to go to work. She takes her work very seriously.

Later she texts me that when she left that morning, there was a police officer waiting to talk to her. She was very worried about the beach, but nothing ever came of that.

One day I was in a café on the beach in Santa Monica. I was in a meeting with Sara from Qatar, who worked for J. P. Morgan and a man. We were discussing business, but no particular deal.

I saw a young woman in her mid-twenties with her back to me. I looked down and I was horrified to see the shoes on her feet. They were terribly dilapidated, full of holes, and nearly completely gone. They were hardly shoes at all. You could see a nail that should be holding the shoe together protruding from one of them.

I turned to my friends in the meeting and told them how emotionally distressed I was to see this here in Santa Monica. I had grown up very poor myself and sometimes had had no shoes as a child. For this reason, I started a charity called Shoe4Child.org. Shoe4Child.org is a non-profit organization that partners with communities to start up initiatives that promote education and entrepreneurship and strongly believes in communities that are active participants in their own development.

Every human being should have decent shoes to wear. It moved me very much to see this young woman, and I was very worried for her.

I could not stop myself from intervening. I had to do something to help this girl. I had to find out how I could help her. I went over to her to tell her about the nail, because I was worried she would hurt herself. I asked her, "Are these the only shoes you have?" She began to get emotional. I could see tears welling up in her eyes. She started crying and she told me that she was a third-year neuroscience student from New Zealand. I was saddened to hear that someone who was clearly bright and able to study something so difficult and important would have to wear shoes like this.

"Please," I said, "let me take you to a shop to buy some shoes. There must be someplace in this neighborhood where I can buy you some shoes." She refused. I implored her, but she told me that she was leaving that day for the airport to go back to New Zealand.

Then she asked me if I was able to drive her to the airport, as her friend who was supposed to drop her off was not responding to her calls. I told her I would take her to the airport but first I must drop Sarah at Sunset Boulevard where she had left her car. I was driving the SL550 so I wasn't able to place three passengers in my car, as the car is made only for a driver and one passenger.

I asked her to wait for me and bought her a bottle of water. Then I left with Sara to drop her on Sunset Strip.

I wasn't aware of the traffic jam driving from Santa Monica to Sunset. It took me an hour and another hour to return. Altogether, I spent more than two hours on the road, which I thought would be less than an hour. Sadly, when I came back to the coffee shop, she was not there.

It is unfortunate that I didn't ask for her phone number. I just didn't want to make the impression that I had personal interest in her by asking her number. My intention was purely to help her and I thought it would take me less than an hour!

■ ■ ■

Percy introduces me to Larissa. Larissa is a very sweet person, kind and attentive to the needs of those she is close to. She has a lot of high-level negotiation skills, which she puts to use in her business and in her personal life. She acts like a counselor to her friends, listening to them and helping them to solve their problems. Larissa has also been an angel in my life. Larissa is a deeply empathetic and caring person, and when she heard my story, she took both of my hands in hers and told me that she wanted the best for me and for Naomi.

As a trusted friend, I told her all about what Naomi and I had been through, through such a long period of time, and about the forces that blocked us and kept us from our happiness. For a time, Larisa tried to negotiate with Naomi for me. She likes me so much and she really wants me to be happy.

It was with Larissa and Percy that I finally met Dick

Michaels. One day I get a call from Percy. Dick Michaels has a movie project he would like to make happen, and he wants to include all of us in the project. We went for a lunch meeting in West Hollywood at a high-end health food restaurant. The vibe was casual, with rough-hewn wood and tiny plants everywhere. On the menu, everything was avocado, almonds, quinoa, blueberries, sushi-grade fish, kale, and plated photo-ready. Very Los Angeles. There were celebrities there just a few tables away, but it's always best not to stare.

In Los Angeles, you have to be as cool as everyone else, and people will respect you. In the meeting with us is a young man named Ross who runs a multibillion-dollar fund that finances movies and other creative projects. There was another guy from MGM, who was from the UK originally. The representative from MGM tells me that he wants to work with me. He is not the first person in the movie industry to say this to me. I am beginning to see that industry people in Los Angeles admire me and see a very bright future for me here.

Once again, Percy was being gruff and intimidating, souring the atmosphere of the meeting for everyone else. I got upset again and told him I didn't like what was happening. I told Percy I wasn't paying the bill this time, since he was acting like that. I told him I wouldn't drive him home either. He would have to get a ride somewhere else.

He started mocking me and deriding my dispute with the Swiss government. He told me that I was ridiculous to want an apology.

"I don't want an apology!" I snapped at him. "I just want to live my life and do my business deals without being blocked by them."

It is such a natural thing to want. If anyone is foolish, it is Percy for not seeing that. I suspect that he is jealous of my success and my widely recognized business acumen.

He looks at me, big and tough again, and says, "You are a dead man."

Larissa is very shocked. She is a kind person and she is not used to this type of talk. She does not want me to have any conflict with Percy because he presents himself as such a dangerous man. She cares about me, and is a real friend. Needless to say, that project did not end up happening because of the way that Percy behaved. I decided to limit my contact with Percy if possible. He is making more trouble than he is worth to me.

A few days after that, I was driving my Mercedes-Benz SL550 through Hollywood. It was starting to rain. When I stopped at a corner, I saw an older man carrying some files. I looked closely at him, thinking that I would stop to give him a ride. I try to do things like this whenever I can. Once I looked closer, I saw that it was Dick Michaels, whom I had met in that earlier meeting with the

MGM people.

I pulled my car over next to him and greeted him warmly. He was surprised, I think, that someone would do that. He didn't remember me at first but then as we talked it dawned on him who I was. He was very warm and friendly, saying how much it warmed his heart that I would stop to help him. Not a lot of people in Los Angeles would do that, he said. "Ah, well, I am not a lot of people," I laughed. I took him to his car and helped him load the files into the trunk. We chatted for a little while about our mutual business interests and we exchanged cards.

■ ■ ■

The next day, I called up Dick. He had mentioned a business deal for which he was seeking investors. To be honest, it wasn't something I ordinarily invest in, but I wanted to build our relationship. When you have a deal you want to make, it is always good to talk to people about it in order to refine your ideas with other smart businesspeople.

If you have a business associate or contact who has an idea to talk to you about, it is similarly a good idea to take the meeting with them and listen. Your time is not wasted in supporting your friend. This is how business relationships are built. This is how you know which friends have which talents so that you can assemble a team down

TARIKU BOGALE

the road and signal to others that you have talents to offer them, too. This kind of openness to conversation builds relationships, and that leads to success. That is another pro tip from my decades of experience.

After this meeting, Dick and I got to spending time together, having lunch regularly. He is the kind of friend an angel had clearly sent me, because he is always so generous with his knowledge of Hollywood and his contacts. He knows all the major players at the big studios and he knew many important smaller players, too, that were interested in new projects.

More importantly, everyone in Hollywood knew about the quality of his work and trusted his judgment and reputation. He takes his senior status seriously enough that he knew what he had and he shared what he could, but he is also a regular guy, as they say, jovial and good-natured in his outlook.

I mentioned earlier that Dick had had an intense love affair with Elizabeth Montgomery at the height of her stardom. Like me, he likes beautiful women and they like him. He likes to be out on the town in Hollywood, enjoying the glamorous life. I think it gave him some pleasure to bring me along to those meetings, parties, and premieres and to introduce me to a Hollywood world that I was experiencing for the first time.

One day he called me up and asked if I had a tuxedo.

212

I told him that my tuxedo was in South Africa. He said, "Well, in that case, you must go out right away and buy a tuxedo without delay. There is no time to waste." His voice became low, confidential, playful. It thrummed with excitement. "Tomorrow night you will accompany me to the Egyptian Theatre for the premiere of *Mansion of Blood*.

"Prepare yourself to be a central participant in the most elegant of affairs. You will not be disappointed. You will need to find a suit *tout de suite* and have it properly fitted. Please call me once you find one so I won't worry that you have it. I will tell you everything you need to know so that you can make a truly grand entrance at your first Hollywood premiere. You *are going to love* it."

That was the beginning of my journey to stardom and my first step toward popular recognition as the next James Bond.

CHAPTER FIFTEEN:

A Socialite's Butterfly and a Monarch: Making a Splash with Hollywood and European Royalty

WHEN I GOT off the phone with Dick, I dressed quickly but carefully for a day of take-no-prisoners shopping in Los Angeles' Rodeo Drive fashion boutiques. Dick gave me the name of one of Los Angeles' most sought-after tailors, a very talented older Russian woman who only took new clients on recommendation from trusted old ones. The tailor accepted my request to become a client and assured me that she would do any alterations the shop could not provide on short notice, at a premium price, of course. My Tom Ford sunglasses shading my shining eyes from the California sun, I hopped into my Mercedes Benz SL550 and headed out to find the perfect classic tux and all the accessories to go with it.

While I knew that it was possible to rent a tux, Dick Michaels had hinted that this would be the first but certainly not the only red carpet event I would be attending. As I shopped for just the right cut, his advice on how a proper celebrity acts on the red carpet echoed in my ears.

Remember, Derick, he instructed me, *when you are on the red carpet you are there to be the center of attention, admired by all who stand outside the carpet, photographed and filmed for magazines, newspapers, television, and Internet news sites.*

People on the red carpet do not take selfies. When you are on the red carpet you are there to be in the pictures taken by paparazzi and admiring onlookers, not to take pictures yourself.

The eye of the camera is upon you, so don't even think of taking out your own camera! You may certainly admire the glamorous ensembles of others in attendance, particularly when it is their turn to make a grand entrance, but like a true star, when you make your entrance in style, you command attention, you do not pay it out.

He certainly had my attention with these instructions. He smiled at me wryly and added with a twinkle in his eye, *Somehow I don't think you'll have any trouble commanding anyone's attention.* We chuckled together at his little joke. He knew from experience already that I turned heads wherever we went!

Dick Michaels had introduced me to a movie studio executive friend who suggested that I look into working with a public relations professional, as it was becoming clear that already I was making a splash in Hollywood and would need consultants to help me manage my image. Hollywood is an image business, quite literally in the sense that every day in print media and online, there are new photographs and videos of celebrities doing everything from attending elegant events to going to the shops or coming from brunch and yoga classes.

Dick Michaels introduced me to a very high-level PR executive, whose name was Neil. When I told Jennifer about Neil, she said that he was the from the biggest, most important PR firm and only handled elite clients. Neil handled A-list celebrities and worked for Warner Brothers. Dick Michaels invited me to his office for a meeting with Neil to discuss having Neil represent me. He told me that he saw my seriousness and my direction. He admired all the work I have done and saw very much potential for us to move forward.

Following that Neil began to invite me to high-end events, of the sort that his clients usually attend. He was connecting me with other elite people in the center of Hollywood social life, already helping me to move further into this world that I clearly belonged in. One particularly memorable event was the exclusive "Evening in the Clouds" event featuring a glamorous dinner served outside on a ranch at sunset, with a special performance by the world-class performer John Legend. I had no idea how special this event would be until I arrived. Dick Michaels texted me saying that Neil wanted to invite me to an extraordinary event. I smiled when I received this text, anticipating something truly special. Dick did not disappoint me. He never does.

We were taken early in the day via limousine out to the desert to the Golden Oak Ranch in Santa Clarita. The event was sponsored by Stella Artois, a beautiful dinner of California cuisine. Everyone looked glamorous in the desert light. It was truly creative and spectacular to hold this event outdoors with the gorgeous backdrop of a desert ranch.

In our group were all of Neil's friends, many of them beautiful women. They were all media people and all knew one another. I was the only new person, and as the new person, they were very kind to me, inviting me into their conversations. We had a wonderful time together, a lot of fun. One of the men there was a famous journalist—I'm afraid I cannot reveal his name here—and he knew of me by reputation. He was very pleased to make my acquaintance. It was a red carpet media event, and I was given a media badge, though I sat with the rest of the guests. Everyone was good looking, successful, part of the Hollywood scene, and out to enjoy a special kind of event together that only the Hollywood elite could access. Neil was introducing me to the media already.

The tables were long and white, facing perpendicular to a small white stage. On the stage was a beautiful white baby grand piano. They announced John Legend and everyone clapped appreciatively in anticipation. He came and played an exclusive concert, a tiny concert suitable for a dinner party, and I was a member of that special group invited to the show. Everyone there looked good, laughing and talking, enjoying the music, the beautiful food, the incredible setting, and the drinks from Stella Artois. John Legend played only five songs, just for us. The event cost $500,000.

At the center of the entertainment after the dinner was a hot-air balloon in bright rainbow colors. This was the reason for the title "Evening in the Clouds." Guests took turns riding in the balloon over the desert landscape. When my turn came, I was inside the woven basket of the balloon alone, with film cameras focused on me, following my journey over the panorama. The moment as I ascended and soared was being captured for posterity. Neil was clearly a very smart and well-connected person. The game was to plug me in to the right social scenes and drop me like a parachute jumper into the center of media attention.

I loved the event. I loved the food. I loved the glamour. And everyone there said they loved being there with me. I could tell that there would be big things coming for me, over the horizon.

You always have to look your best, even if it's a casual look, in your gym clothes, and if you don't manage your image there is no telling what the press may make of it. Good image management means a good reputation, possibly a growing following, and that translates into success. It's very different from the business world, but as I've said before, I like new challenges. That's where the fun is in life! Trying new things and conquering new worlds. I have the heart of a lion, the king of the jungle, I am often told, so I am always out to conquer more!

My PR consultant, Edward Lozzi, inspected my new tuxedo, shirt, shoes, and tie. He paid attention even to my cufflinks (Tiffany, a gift from a past lover) and my socks (Paul Smith). I appreciate it when someone has an eye for detail. It's something I look for in my staff. In Edward's case this eye for detail was about making me look as polished and perfect as could be for the premiere entrance of Derick Bogale! I am sure people thought it was the movie that was having its Hollywood premiere, but that night, it would also be me! The beautiful people and the film industry of Hollywood, it was becoming increasingly clear, were ready for me to join them.

Allow me to backtrack so that you understand what I mean. Long before this night, there had been signs that I would soon be joining the glittering stars in the glow of the movie lights. One night, some months back, I was dining alone at Le Petit Four on Sunset Strip. I was seated at the banquette, looking out at the restaurant, savoring every bite of my ahi tuna steak, seared to perfection.

A charming young woman near me met my eye and held up her glass of white wine in a gesture of a toast when I smiled back. I held mine up in return and we each took a sip. A few minutes passed as we each attended to our own food, lost in our own thoughts. When I looked up again, she lifted her glass to me. When I went to lift mine, it was nearly empty. I pouted, in a playfully exaggerated expression of sadness at my rapidly dwindling drink. She held up her chilled bottle of Meursault and spoke for the first time. "*Dommage!*" she said in French. "Why don't you share some of mine, then? It's perfectly chilled and there's plenty left for two." Her eyes flashed flirtatiously.

"Oh, I cannot possibly!" I demurred out of sheer politeness, for of course I would enjoy nothing more than to share a drink and a meal with a lovely young woman rather than continue to eat alone.

"Please. I insist," she said, and with a playful grin, she got up from her chair and brought the bottle over to me.

I laughed at her audacity. "Very well, but you must join me, then."

I made a mental note to tell the server that I would be picking up her check as well. She immediately launched into a story about an art show she had just attended, or maybe it was a party in the Hamptons? Clearly she was someone who got around a lot to the best parties.

I beamed broadly at her and took it all in, her chattering friendliness, her clear connections to the crème de la crème of social life on both American coasts. As she leaned toward me conspiratorially to drop a morsel of movie gossip (my lawyer tells me it is too dangerous to share, I'm sorry to say), I saw her scarf slip to reveal more of her tattoo: a beautiful butterfly in flight. She came to the end of her story, which was simply as delicious as the French wine, and her laughter sparkled like a thousand tiny camera flashes in the distance. "I'm Nikki, by the way," she added almost as an afterthought, "Nikki Spielberg."

Her smile was a little crooked when she was playing, her head a little cocked to the left when she told a story. She could be almost any charming young woman then, engaging my attention. But the signs of the glamorous life she led—the most lavish parties, the most expensive high fashion, private jets, yachts, nightclubs in every city, and vacations on every exclusive island resort—were all around her, always.

She lived among those things as if they were ordinary, though her pleasure and constant glow showed that surely they were anything but. She shared a last name, of course, with her Hollywood superstar director uncle, and that was not lost on me or on anyone else. I wondered what the universe was telling me, sending a delightful angel named *Spielberg* to my table with a gift of convivial conversation and delicious chilled French wine? Surely it was a sign of welcoming.

What did this mean for my future? I knew it had to be a sign of good things to come, of big things. A butterfly, after all, undergoes a transformation, and is prized for its exquisite beauty and uniqueness among creatures. The most famous butterfly is the monarch. A monarch is, as everyone knows, the royal leader, a king or queen enthroned in all splendor, admired by his or her subjects and caring for them. Living the best, most exciting kind of life. Would that be in store for me, in Hollywood? The best, most exciting kind of life among the upper echelons of the elite?

Nikki and I went everywhere together after that. We went to the Shutters on the Beach Hotel in Santa Monica and had dinner with friends. She loved to drink cocktails and always knew where a new spot was opening with the most expert bartenders. The cameras would be there, too, sometimes press but also for the selfies she liked to take with her friends, having a good time. I enjoyed it, and she seemed intrigued by me.

We had a mutual interest in fashion, and I was pleased to hear that I had also been in attendance at LA's recent Fashion Week.

"Maybe that's why I felt so comfortable talking to you at first," she mused. "I must have seen you at some of the parties and shows."

I told her about the charity I started for homeless people after I saw how many homeless there were outside of the Fashion Week locations downtown. I think she was very interested to hear about my work in international business. As a socialite, she mostly went to art shows and parties and wasn't involved in business like I was.

Nikki loved the art world, and it loved her back. She was always invited to art parties, as well as parties for magazines and other cultural institutions. I think she liked having me go with her because we always looked so good together. We went to the exclusive opening night party of an art exhibit hosted by *Rolling Stone* magazine, a very glamorous party.

At one party, in Soho, we were actually not on the list that night, but we managed to evade security and get inside through a side entrance. She liked to get into a little trouble like that, in a harmless kind of way. Nothing serious, but she had a mischievous side, and as in a lot of areas, we fed off of each other.

Once inside, I met a guy who worked for one of the major studios. We got to talking and he gave me his card. He told me that he would be very pleased to have lunch with me to discuss my plans in Hollywood. I had started talking to Dick about scripts and I had a few ideas I was ready to shop around.

Sometimes when Nikki and I went out together, I could see that people were trying to separate us. I didn't understand this, since we had planned to go out that night together, and we had arrived together, but it was happening. People were systematically trying to keep us apart. I wondered also what that meant, that just as in New York, and in Zurich as well, people in Los Angeles were trying to block me from my happiness.

Nikki was just a friend to me, nothing more, but I still cared about her and enjoyed her company. She quite obviously enjoyed mine. Why would this happen? Would this kind of thing continue to pop up and stand in my way as I climbed the glittering stairway to stardom?

After becoming friends with Nikki Spielberg, and attracting the attention of movie executives at nightclubs, it made good sense that I would go with Dick Michaels to the Hollywood premiere of *Mansion of Blood* at Grauman's Egyptian Theatre. Situated on Hollywood Boulevard, the Egyptian, as everyone called it, was a historic theater from the 1920s and a monument to the glamour of that earlier golden era of American movie history. Dick and I arrived at just the right time. "Not too late, and not too early," he stressed, and I smiled. I liked that Dick always knew the correct way to do things in Hollywood.

On the red carpet, all of the guests in evening wear took their turns arriving and being photographed for the movie's publicity.

"Who are you? You look so sharp, like James Bond!" one photographer exclaimed. Not everyone had the good taste to come in a tuxedo. In the beautiful and perfectly fitted suit I had purchased, I had a level of polish that made me stand out even from a Hollywood crowd.

"Definitely," agreed another one. "The camera loves you. The next Double Oh Seven is here tonight!"

The movie was in the horror genre, which isn't one of my favorites, but it was exciting to sit in that ornate, gilded room with Hollywood high society and to once again have signs point to a future as a movie star.

James Bond, I thought. *Yes, I could do that. I could certainly do that.*

Was it obvious that I had spent years in international circles, surrounded by mystery and intrigue? Did people know about the threats I had survived from the taxi gangsters in Johannesburg, about the government opposition I withstood in Switzerland, about the powerful South African politicians I stood up to, about the oppressed human rights activist I had harbored and counseled in Ethiopia? Did they know about my deportation or about my imprisonment in Dar es Salaam, or about my careful diplomatic maneuverings? Did they know that I was the rare man who had the guts to stand up to a cleaner? Or did I simply wear those characteristics on my face, as easily and as elegantly as I wore my hand-tailored suit?

I had always been a businessman and a philanthropist, but now I was beginning to see what new avenues might open up to me in California, and as someone who loves new and exciting things, I have to say, I liked the idea very much.

At the after party for *Mansion of Blood*, there were of course delicious cocktails served in shining glassware by waiters in white jackets carrying trays. There were tables set with white tablecloths and at the front there was a band.

All of the attending guests drank and danced and laughed. For a moment I thought I might have gone back in time to 1920s Hollywood. Or perhaps the ghosts of that era, such as John Barrymore and Douglas Fairbanks, were smiling down on me.

As we mingled with the crowd, Dick would tell me little things about the people we met. This one was an important casting agent. That one was close to the editor of *Variety*. The next had worked at the E! Television network.

I collected business cards and handed mine out all night. I met an engaging young woman named Priscilla, a singer, who gave me her number before leaving.

After I finished talking to Priscilla, an elegantly dressed German woman in a pale green silk gown came over to me. I think people were drawn to this unknown person, new in town, so well turned out in a proper tuxedo, but hidden behind classic movie star sunglasses.

The German woman looked strikingly like Naomi, and the resemblance as well as the accent they both had when they spoke English made me take in my breath sharply, though I hid my surprise from her well. Her name was Marieke, and she was there with her own personal security detail. I heard whispers behind me. When Marieke wasn't within earshot, another acquaintance casually mentioned that she was in fact descended from royalty.

The well-dressed man with her was her brother, also a royal, who showed me his ID to show that he is a prince from Germany. Marieke came over toward me again, beckoning the waiter as she walked. She took two champagne flutes from the tray, handed me one, and whispered: would I dance with her after this drink?

Her friend Clarissa was growing tired and wanted to go home, but Marieke was hoping to spend more time with me. Her princely brother kept coming over to us and taking Marieke away. She wanted to send Clarissa home but it was clear to me that her brother did not want to leave Marieke there alone with me.

I wondered again about European elites and their seeming constant need to keep women away from me. It was confusing, and it very nearly soured the party for me.

■ ■ ■

I chose to pay it no mind. Already two Hollywood professionals had told me that they thought I would be the next James Bond! Here I was a center of attention at a Hollywood premiere in the most historic of Los Angeles movie theaters.

My PR rep, Edward Lozzi, complimented me on the red carpet photos. Dick Michaels, a distinguished elder statesman of the entertainment industry, was on my side, happily advising me, guiding my progress, inviting me to the best parties, and helping me arrange meetings to plan my projects. I had met and been befriended by Nikki Spielberg, and while in her rarified orbit I was approached regularly by studio executives and consultants who were showing a very real interest in my plans.

Perhaps the meaning of Nikki's butterfly tattoo was that, being transformed into the next James Bond, I would become a kind of royalty in my own right, different from what existed in old-world Europe. Marieke was beautiful and elegant enough, but that world I had left behind in Zurich suddenly seemed a million miles away from sunny southern California.

Another important person from my time in Los Angeles, is Miguel, my lawyer. Miguel is a celebrity lawyer, and it would be enough for many people to know who

I meant even if I only say his first name. He is a subtle man, but a man of many connections, and a very sharp lawyer. I met Miguel through George. George is Jennifer's associate partner, the Rodeo Drive real estate agent. All of Jennifer's properties and clientele are very exclusive and her family is very connected, including her associate partner.

People gain in prestige when they introduce a new, prestigious person to their friend and colleague. This is one way that networking works among successful people. Successful people are always interested in expanding their networks because new people can add fresh energy as well as new possibilities. I always recommend taking an expansive view of your network when I advise young people starting out in business. For this reason, Miguel was very excited to meet me, just as I was pleased to meet him. And as it happened, he gained in me a new client who would give him plenty of work, as well as a new friend to show off on the Los Angeles social scene.

It was a very strategic move for me to take on Miguel as my lawyer, for reasons that you will see. It turned out that I would need the best representation I could get because there were still people who wished to block my progress and success. It is hard to fathom why but mysteriously there would still appear forces that would try to prevent me from fulfilling my dreams and destiny. I am a peaceful warrior for my causes, for my own success, and for the success of others I wish to inspire, and for the success of those who work with me. I only put positive things into the world, so it is very strange that so many forces conspire to keep me from my destiny.

My lawyer, Miguel, had suggested that I apply under the special provision for only the most talented people. This kind of green card was the same kind given to Albert Einstein. It is for people who have talents and special expertise and status unlike almost any other in the world. Miguel assured me that I should be a shoe-in for this green card. It should only take a few days. Most people have to wait years for a green card. But with my record in business, my standing in the international community, my schooling in Zurich, and the billions of dollars of deals I was invited to take part in, I was a natural candidate.

It was a snap decision, based on my gut instinct. I have a very strong feeling about people, and when someone makes a strong impression on me, I act fast. That may not work for everyone. It may be one of the special talents I have in business and in life, to see very quickly into the spirt and mind of another person. Miguel also saw into my mind, he later told me. He saw that star quality that helped propel me in business that would also push me ahead in Hollywood.

Because of this special relationship, Miguel was always glad to introduce me to other people. Among them was Eduardo. Like a lot of people I met in Los Angeles, Eduardo was young, successful, and very stylish. He had once been a model for the Hugo Boss fashion line. What stood out to him was that we had something else in common, something very important to both of us, and that was our commitment to the charities and causes we each cared about. We bonded over this. He was impressed with my commitment to helping children in Africa with no shoes, homeless people in Los Angeles, and to inspire young people all over the world by telling my story. He was amazed at the things I had seen in my life! At the place where my story had begun and the world that I opened up for myself! He agreed that had I made different choices, I could easily have kept my world very small or could have turned to drugs or other forms of criminality and destruction strictly for me own gain.

Having formed this bond one night over a convivial dinner hosted by Miguel, Eduardo invited me to an event in downtown Los Angeles. The event was a glamorous charity gala for an organization fighting sex trafficking. There were many beautiful people there, smiling for their photographs and eating exquisite bites of food brought by impeccable waiters. We drank champagne that night, and I made some very important connections. It felt very good to take a stand against something as despicable as sex trafficking. In the VIP area, where Eduardo had taken me, we talked of the movie Eduardo had produced, called Little Boy. He had many years of experience in Hollywood, and like Dick Michaels was kind enough to open even more doors for me. He took me across the room to introduce me to Pierce Brosnan and former Mexican president Vicente Fox and we greeted each other warmly. Either the angels were watching over me, or he saw something special in me, too. It is good fortune like this that makes me committed to fulfilling my destiny.

Pierce Brosnan, as everyone knows, played James Bond. Here was yet another signal that such a role would come my way soon! Bond is the kind of role that is only given to the most stylish of men, and they are all men who retain that sense of style and class long after they pass the role on to the next big star. That night, Pierce met my eye with his characteristic twinkle, and tilted his head slightly. He warmly clasped my hand, and after a pause, walked away from me with an astonishing smile. I thought perhaps I saw him wink at that moment, but I can't be sure. I could feel in the conversation that he knew he was meeting a fellow James Bond, someone already living a life of international intrigue amid luxurious amenities, glamorous cars, and the most beautiful women.

Soon after this, Dick Michaels arranged a meeting with a former Paramount president who was interested in my story. I had my writer write up a treatment showing the high points of the many adventures I had had and obstacles I had overcome so far. All of this at such a young age! The Paramount producer was impressed. He laid out a budget for me: it would cost $250 million to make this movie. I was angry at first, and felt he was trying to discourage me, but later I realized he was being realistic. I would have to rent an office and he would have to work full time. We would need a full staff. I began to understand a bit more how Hollywood worked.

It was at this time in Los Angeles that someone slipped a photograph of Charlize Theron under my door. Someone wanted to put her into my mind. As it happens, Charlize Theron is South African, of course. Perhaps whoever was thinking of putting her into my mind was thinking of that connection. Perhaps it was also that we were both in Hollywood and working in movies, though of course I was just starting out in movies after having made my fortune and name as a global businessperson. I decided to look her up on the Internet to see what she was doing.

It turned out that she was breaking up with Sean Penn! Charlize was also a member at the Chateau Marmont. I was not a member there, yet, but Miguel would often make reservations for me. It was tantalizing to see that we had these things in common, and here she was, slipped under my door so subtly one day. What did this mean? And just after being escorted to meet Pierce Brosnan!

I felt a rush of adventure and possibility as my head filled with dreams. I decided to see if I could tease the public and the press just a bit by dropping some hints, and I posted a picture of myself as James Bond on my LinkedIn and my Facebook. Much to my surprise, Idris Elba commented on my Facebook! He wrote that I was an imposter! Clearly, I had touched a nerve. He could see that something was developing for me, and wanted to stake a claim to his ground. This was more interesting than no reaction at all.

It was becoming more and more clear during this time in Los Angeles that I would soon settle there. So many signs, great and small, were pointing to my future as the next James Bond. There were deals that I was invited to consider. I was taking a lot of important meetings with high-powered people. The California sun was shining on me, and like many before me, promising me fame and good fortune. Who was I to turn away from that?

I had stood up to endless challenges. However, I continued on to fulfill my dreams again and again despite far larger obstacles. Nothing can possibly get in the way of my happiness and success, I told myself, because I am unstoppable.